# Scats
# and
# Tracks
## of

---

## North America

---

*A Field Guide to the Signs of Nearly 150
Wildlife Species*

James C. Halfpenny, Ph.D.

Illustrated by Todd Telander

**FALCON**GUIDES ®

GUILFORD, CONNECTICUT
HELENA, MONTANA

AN IMPRINT OF THE GLOBE PEQUOT PRESS

# FALCONGUIDES®

Maps created by James C. Halfpenny, Ph.D. © Morris Book Publishing, LLC

Library of Congress Catalgoing-in-Publication Data

Halfpenny, James C.
  Scats and tracks of North America: a field guide to the signs of nearly 150 wildlife species / James C. Halfpenny ; illustrated by Todd Telander.

  p. cm. -- (Scats and tracks series)
Includes bibliographical references and index.
ISBN 978-0-7627-4842-6
1. Animal tracks--North America. I. Title
QL768.H353 2008
591.97--dc22

                                            2008018579

Printed in the United States of America
10 9 8 7 6 5

*To Diann, my alpha partner, ursophile, and tracking friend,*
*for all her loving support and help.*

*JH*

# Contents

Acknowledgments . . . . . . . . . . . . . . . . . . . . . . . . . . . .vii

Introduction . . . . . . . . . . . . . . . . . . . . . . . . . . . . . . . . .1

About tracking . . . . . . . . . . . . . . . . . . . . . . . . . . . . . . .3

    Field notes and preserving tracks . . . . . . . . . . . . . .3

    Scats and bird pellets . . . . . . . . . . . . . . . . . . . . . . . .6

    Anatomy and footprint nomenclature . . . . . . . . . . .8

    Track measurements . . . . . . . . . . . . . . . . . . . . . . . .10

    Gaits and trails . . . . . . . . . . . . . . . . . . . . . . . . . . .12

    Trail measurements . . . . . . . . . . . . . . . . . . . . . . . .16

Glossary of terms . . . . . . . . . . . . . . . . . . . . . . . . . . . .18

How to use *Scats and Tracks* . . . . . . . . . . . . . . . . .23

    Illustrations . . . . . . . . . . . . . . . . . . . . . . . . . . . . . .23

    How to use the track accounts . . . . . . . . . . . . . . . .23

Visual key to tracks . . . . . . . . . . . . . . . . . . . . . . . . . .26

Scats and Tracks of North America

    Invertebrates: Fiddler and horseshoe crabs . . . . . .30

    Amphibians: Newts, salamanders,
        toads, and frogs . . . . . . . . . . . . . . . . . . . . . . . .34

    Reptiles: Lizards, turtles, and snakes . . . . . . . . . . .52

    Avians: Birds . . . . . . . . . . . . . . . . . . . . . . . . . . . . .70

    Marsupial: Opossum . . . . . . . . . . . . . . . . . . . . . .142

    Insectivores: Shrews . . . . . . . . . . . . . . . . . . . . . . .144

    Armadillo . . . . . . . . . . . . . . . . . . . . . . . . . . . . . .146

    Canids: Foxes, coyotes, and wolves . . . . . . . . . . .148

    Felids: Mountain lions, bobcats, and relatives . . .160

Ursids: Bears. . . . . . . . . . . . . . . . . . . . . . . . . . . 172

Procyonids: Ringtails, coatis, and raccoons . . . . .180

Mustelids: Weasels and relatives. . . . . . . . . . . . .186

Lagomorphs: Rabbits, hares, and pikas . . . . . . . .206

Rodents: Squirrels, mice,
   muskrats, and relatives . . . . . . . . . . . . . . . . . .222

Hoofed mammals: Deer, caribou,
   sheep, and relatives. . . . . . . . . . . . . . . . . . . . .296

Selected reading . . . . . . . . . . . . . . . . . . . . . . . . . .322

Index. . . . . . . . . . . . . . . . . . . . . . . . . . . . . . . . . . .324

About the author . . . . . . . . . . . . . . . . . . . . . . . . . .328

About the illustrator. . . . . . . . . . . . . . . . . . . . . . . .328

# Acknowledgments

First and foremost, I wish to thank all my students for their years of questions and help, but most of all for the time we've shared tracking and studying in the field. I also wish to thank Tim Benner, Sara Boles, Jen Broom, Sarah Broom, Jim Bruchac, Don Clark, Greg Cook, Deborah Cowman, Bill Desmarais, Alice Droske, Mark Elbroch, Tom Ellison, June Emerson, Steve Engel, Bob Evans, Dixie Finley, Lee Fitzhugh, Louise Forrest, Mark Gleason, Jim Hammill, Sue Lane, Louis Liebenberg, Tom Lindsay, Jim Lowery, Larry Marlow, Terry Mc-Eneany, Dorothy Mcleer, Marvin Miller, Sue Morse, Mardy Murie, Olas Murie, Murie Museum, Patrick Nagi, Gary Norris, Judy Norris, John Olson, Lance Peck, Belinda Peck, Rolf Peterson, Paul Rezendes, Beth Rogers, John Rogers, Ron Schultz, Tim Schaub, Jim Scott, Marty Silver, Justin Steventon, Phil Tanimoto, Dave Tiller, Eric Trott, Pam Troxell, Teton Science School, Vince Walsch, Al Warren, Nancy Warren, Adrian Wydeven, and Jon Young. I also give thanks to Jim Bruchac, co-author of *Scats and Tracks of the Northeast, Scat and Tracks of the Mid-Atlantic,* and *Scats and Tracks of the Southeast,* for the great times we've shared tracking!

JH

# Introduction

In the late 1970s the era of watchable wildlife arrived in the United States. Baby boomers wanted to turn to and experience the outdoors. Television brought wildlife closer than ever. Bird-watching thrived. Now more than ever, millions of people want to watch wild animals. Wildlife are not always easy to find and observe, though. Finding their tracks and signs is an exciting alternative to actually seeing the animals. Trackable wildlife adds another dimension to the outdoor experience. Todd and I wish to share that dimension, the joy of reading stories written in the soil and snow.

Upwards of ten books on tracking have been written in the United States during each decade of the twentieth century and this first decade of the twenty-first. In *Scats and Tracks of North America*, I focus on the continent of North America north of Mexico, with details about the most common or characteristic species of mammals, birds, reptiles, and amphibians. (I have included a few rare species because of their particular interest or significance. For example, what a coup it would be to document a jaguarundi, polar bear, or wolverine.) We've intentionally limited the number of species covered in order to keep the information manageable.

As your knowledge and interest in tracking grows, you may want to find additional information and help. Key references are listed in Selected Reading. For a more detailed investigation of tracking, I recommend my book *A Field Guide to Mammal Tracking in North America* (1986, Johnson Publishing, Boulder, Colorado), and titles by Olaus Murie, Louise R. Forrest, Mark Elbroch, and Paul Rezendes.

My organization will, in computer parlance, provide interactive access to expand your tracking background. A Naturalist's World (ANW), directed by myself, is an ecologically oriented company dedicated to providing educational programs and materials reflecting the natural history of North America. Diann Thompson and I run the daily business, teach classes, and lead programs. Our on-site classes provide hands-on experience and in-depth information about animals, their tracks, and the ecology of their environments. In addition to tracking classes, our field programs cover the behavior of bears, wolves, winter ecology, the northern lights, and alpine ecology. ANW also provides books, videos, slide shows, and computer programs for self-study and as teaching and field aids. You can check out ANW on the Internet at www.tracknature.com. Class schedules, product information, and information about ANW can be obtained from P.O. Box 989, Gardiner, MT 59030, phone (406) 848-9458, or on the Web at www.tracknature.com and www.trackinganimals.net.

And please check out the Ndakinna Wilderness Project directed by Jim Bruchac. Ndakinna offers tracking classes and adventures for all ages. Information can be obtained by writing to 23 Middle Grove Road, Greenfield Center, NY 128333; calling (518) 583-9980; or visiting www.ndakinna.com.

Keep on tracking!

—*James C. Halfpenny*

# About tracking

Tracking is for everyone—beginner and expert, young and old. The fun of nature's challenge is solving the mystery written in the trail. Prepare yourself by learning the background and basics of tracking before exercising your skills in the field.

## Field notes and preserving tracks

To the natural history detective, the track and trail are things of great beauty and significance. They tell part of the story of an animal's life. Tracks and trails deserve to be preserved, both to increase your knowledge and as a record you can share with others. Preservation is commonly made in the form of written notes, casts, or photographs.

Perhaps the most important item in the naturalist's tool kit is the field notebook. Field notes can jog the memory and facilitate better retention of knowledge. The notes can be analyzed later and can be preserved as records of chance encounters. Writing good field notes is an art and a science in itself. Field notes are a source of pride when shown to others and may gain recognition for recording rare and unusual events. And need I mention how quickly memories, especially for details, fade when not preserved?

While great and complex systems have been designed for complete and accurate records, there are really but three requirements for the tracker: ruler, paper, and pen. With these, every trail becomes a record for later analysis and sharing. I cannot emphasize enough the importance of enhancing your tracking experience by keeping notes to which you can later refer!

A simple 3-by-5-inch notebook and a 6-inch ruler are adequate to get started. Use a pencil or a pen with ink that won't run if your notes get wet. To facilitate taking notes, A Naturalist's World produces a waterproof notebook that contains information about footprint groups, gaits, and how to track; data sheets for recording information; and English and metric rulers imprinted on the back cover. See the Introduction for contact information for A Naturalist's World.

Tracks may also be preserved by photographing and making casts. Good photographs can be made by any modern camera that can take a good close-up. When taking pictures, try to fill the viewfinder with the footprint. Get as close as possible. Always include a ruler or some other object in the photo to provide a sense of scale. Avoid using hats, gloves, hands, or objects without a straight edge; round edges do not lend themselves to making accurate measurements from a photo. To avoid distortion, take the photograph from directly above the track, shooting straight down. Also, step back and take photographs of the trail to show the footprints that were photographed close-up. Fast films (ASA of 200 or higher) are generally best because tracks are often found in dark places, especially ground surfaces. Modern digital cameras take excellent photographs that can easily be e-mailed to others.

Plaster casts are the old standby for preserving tracks. I suggest a casting kit that includes a one-quart (one-liter), wide-mouthed plastic jar with a screw lid for carrying dry plaster, a narrow spatula, a plastic mixing cup such as those sold in gas station convenience stores for medium-size drinks, paper for wrapping and transporting the finished cast, and a plastic sack for cleanup. A bottle of water may be needed if water is not available on-site. Two pounds of plaster will make at least four coyote-size track casts.

Purchase plaster from a lumberyard or hardware store, as prices will be more reasonable than at a drugstore or hobby shop. Almost any plaster will work, including plaster of Paris, hydrocal, ultracal, or hydrostone. Avoid getting plaster for wallboard or patching compound, however. These plasters are formulated to be slightly flexible on walls and do not get hard enough for casts. Also avoid PolyPlasters, as they do not set well when the temperature is cooler than 50 degrees Fahrenheit.

Two factors are critical to preventing casts from breaking: thickness and density. In the field, thickness is assured by building a wall around the track to contain the plaster. Natural objects such as twigs, stones, and dirt may be used to make a retaining wall 0.25 to 0.5 inch (0.6 to 1.3 cm) above the track. Alternatively, walls in the form of plastic strips cut from milk cartons or other plastic containers may be taken to the field. Proper density is assured by mixing two parts of plaster to one part of water by volume (read instructions on plaster container) to create a mixture similar in consistency to thick pancake batter or a milk shake.

Place your spatula close to the track, and pour onto the spatula to break the fall of the plaster into the footprint. Working quickly, so the plaster does not set and become too thick, gently pour the plaster first into the fine detailed areas of the footprint and then the rest of the print. Finally, pour the plaster to an appropriate depth (inside the retaining wall) to keep the cast from breaking. Vibrating the spatula up and down across the top of the plaster will cause it to settle evenly and create a smooth back for the cast.

Allow the plaster to dry for 30 minutes, or as long as

is recommended on the plaster package. Gently pick the plaster up by digging your fingers under opposite sides of the cast, and turn the cast over onto one hand. Now wash off the dirt by rubbing the cast with your fingertips under the flowing water of a stream or hose. Do not wash the cast in a sink, as plaster may clog the drain. Let the cast continue to cure for several days in a warm, dry environment. If you need to transport it, wrap the cast in paper. Never wrap the cast in plastic, as trapped moisture may cause it to crumble.

While special techniques are needed for dust and snow, this procedure will allow casting in many situations. Remember, carry a plastic garbage bag, and always clean up your mess. No sign of your plaster should remain to reduce the experience of others who happen by later.

### Scats and bird pellets

Scats and bird pellets (also called cough pellets or castings) are often helpful for identifying an animal or completing the story written in the trail. Scats and pellets help identify not only what the animal was eating but also who the animal was. However, it should be noted that scats and pellets won't help you identify an animal with as much certainty as tracks will. Many animals make similar scats and pellets that are difficult to tell apart.

The scats of many carnivores are very similar, especially when the diet is mostly meat. Size alone does not provide a definitive answer because of the wide range of diameters produced within a species and even by a single member of a species. For example, foxes produce scats ranging in size from 0.3 to 0.8 inch (0.8 to 2.0 cm), coyotes produce scats from 0.5 to 1.3 inches (1.3 to 3.3 cm), and wolves produce scats from 0.5 to 1.5 inches (1.3 to 3.8 cm), and we all know how our own scat varies in size and shape. When judging size, consider both the total quantity of scat and the size of individual pieces. Moist food produces slimmer scats, while fibrous diets produce wider scats.

Given these cautions, scat shapes can be used to identify general groups of animals (see page 9). Spherical shapes flattened top to bottom are deposited by members of the rabbit order. Elongate spheres are deposited by rodents and shrews and, at larger sizes, by deer and their relatives. Long, thick cords are deposited by dogs, bears, and raccoons. Dog scats typically have tapered ends, while those from bears and raccoons are blunt. Cats also produce thick cords with blunt ends, but they tend to be constricted or even broken into short segments. Cords that loop back on themselves are produced by members of the weasel family.

Birds, in general, produce long, thin cords or shapeless, semiliquid excretions. Reptiles and amphibians may produce small elongate spheres or long, thin cords. White, nitrogenous urine deposits—found only on the scats of birds, reptiles, and amphibians—separate them from mammal scats. Scats may be confused with cough pellets. Many bird groups, including owls, raptors, crows, ravens, jays, magpies, gulls, herons, storks, flycatchers, and king-fishers, produce cough pellets in addition to scats. Birds pass digestive juices through what they have eaten to remove the nutrients. Hair, bones, beaks, claws, and other nondigestible parts accumulate in the gizzard (anterior portion of stomach), are compressed, and are coughed up as pellets. Bone and hair remnants in the pellet are easy to identify and tell much about the bird's feeding habits and even the habitats it frequents.

Pellets are grayish in color and are spherical or long and tapered at both ends. When fresh, they are covered by mucus and appear dark black. Pellets are found mainly at roosting sites and nests, and occasionally at feeding areas. They are deposited singly, but many may accumulate beneath a tree where a bird is roosting, nesting, or perching. Nitrogenous scat deposits on the ground or twigs may help verify an object as a pellet. The diameter of the throat determines the maximum diameter of the pellet. In general, large birds produce larger pellets. Shape and diameter allow one to distinguish to some degree among species. Birds generally produce two pellets per day and regurgitate just before taking flight. The time of day when feeding occurred may affect the sample of food items. For example, owls tend to feed on mammals that come out only at night, while hawks feed on animals that are out during daylight hours.

**cough pellet**

### Anatomy and footprint nomenclature

The feet of mammals, birds, reptiles, and amphibians are anatomically complex, and that complexity shows in their footprints. Knowing something of the anatomy of their feet will aid in footprint identification and interpreting trails.

The toes of all animals are numbered from the inside of the foot out (the inside of the foot being the side closest to the animal). Therefore, in humans and other mammals, the thumb or big toe (if present) is number 1 and the little finger or little toe is number 5. In birds, toe 1 (if present) points backward.

Over evolutionary time, toes of animals have become reduced in size or have disappeared altogether. In cats

# Shapes of scats

---

**Spheres**

Rabbits and their relatives

rabbit

---

**Spheres, elongate**

Rodents, shrews, deer, and their relatives

woodrat

shrew

elk

---

**Cords, long and thick**

Wolves, bears, raccoons, and their relatives

coyote

bear

raccoon

---

**Cords, thick and often constricted**

Mountain lions and their relatives

mountain lion

---

**Cords, often folded**

Weasels and their relatives

mink

---

**Cords, long and thin, often with nitrogenous deposits**

Birds, reptiles, and amphibians

Canada goose

lizard

and dogs, toe 1 is absent or reduced to a small toe called a dewclaw.

In deer, elk, sheep, and similar mammals, toe 1 is absent and toes 2 and 5 are reduced and form dewclaws. Toes 3 and 4, the clouts, form the cloven hoof. In pronghorn antelope, toes 1, 2, and 5 are absent. In birds, toe 5 is absent and toe 1 is often reduced and occasionally is absent. In the amphibians covered here, toe 1 has been lost from the front foot.

### Track measurements

To more accurately determine the animal's foot size from its tracks, mountain lion researchers Fjelline and Mansfield (1989) developed what is now called the minimum outline method of measuring tracks.

Place your hand on a hard surface, a table for instance. Note the contact area of your hand with that surface. If your hand went no deeper into that surface, your handprint would have only one size: the minimum outline. If your hand were to sink deeper into the surface—as it would if the surface were, say, mud—it would create a series of variable outlines, each larger than the one before, as the mud flowed around the curved surface of your hand. All footprints have a minimum outline, but only prints that sink into a surface have variable outlines.

Note that while the variable outline of a footprint may only be several millimeters wider than the minimum outline, those few millimeters have a large visual effect. The human eye sees area, and area increases with the square of a linear measurement. In short, a few millimeters of width add a lot of area to a footprint.

The minimum outline size does not change for different surfaces and therefore provides a standard for comparison among surfaces. And though one animal may leave many sizes of footprints depending on surface, slope, and speed, there is only one minimum outline for every footprint that animal might leave. The minimum outline measurement is the only constant and consistent size in tracking.

To measure the minimum outline, study the bottom of a print. The break point where the rounded pad turns upward is the edge of the minimum outline. Use this edge to measure tracks.

Assigning the break point is a subjective judgment, and no two people will always mark it at exactly the same

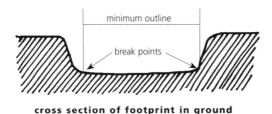

**cross section of footprint in ground**

point. However, testing has shown that an individual tracker using the minimum outline method can reduce personal variation in measurement and that groups of trackers using this method will also become more consistent in their measurement of tracks. Remember the computer rule GIGO: garbage in, garbage out. You cannot get quality measurements from a bad track. Quality measurements are the tracker's goal, and using minimum outline methods greatly reduces exaggeration and variance in measurement.

All measurements in this guide are minimum outline measurements.

The measurements in *Scats and Tracks of North America* are mostly averages gathered from years of tracking. The measurements may not represent your area well, as they are influenced by age, gender, and geographic region. Averages include only animals judged to be adult. However, it is important to remember the great size variation among animals. Every animal was small once in its life, and some never get big. Males are often substantially larger than females. Regional variations in mammal sizes also occur. For example, coyotes are smaller in the southwestern United States and larger in the northeastern part of the country. Their tracks vary accordingly. Therefore, a track in the field may be considerably larger or smaller than the measurements provided. Use track measurements only as a rough guideline, not as an absolute rule. Collect your own database of track measurements for your area.

### Gaits and trails

Coordinated muscle movements result in the various gaits used by animals. In the simplest form, when moving on two legs (bipedal movement), an organism can walk, run, and hop. When moving on four legs (quadrupedal movement), an organism can walk, trot, lope, gallop, bound, and pronk (also called stot). Though other gaits exist, I will confine our discussion to these basic gaits. Each gait leaves a characteristic pattern that may be modified by changes in speed and body angle. The combination of footprints is called the trail. The bipedal walk and run and the

walk    trot

quadrupedal walk and trot result in gaits that are *symmetrical*. The right side of the trail is a mirror image of the left side. The trail patterns for these gaits are the same, alternating right-left pattern, and they differ only by the stride being longer in the run and trot than it is in the walk. In the run and trot, the straddle, the distance from the right edge of the rightmost pad (see page 21) to the left edge of the leftmost pad, also tends to be narrower than it is in the walk.

Quadrupedal movement also results in gaits that are *asymmetrical* (the right half of the trail is not always a mirror image of the left), including lope, gallop, bound, hop, and pronk. These gaits produce patterns that include all four footprints (two fronts, two hinds, two rights, and two lefts) in a group separated from the next group by a space where no footprints appear.

In *gallops*, the feet, front and rear, that move first (or lead) will determine whether the gallop will form a Z-shaped or C-shaped pattern. When the front and hind feet on the same side lead, the pattern takes on a Z shape, called a *transverse* gallop. A right-front lead with a left-hind lead, or vice versa, results in a C-shaped pattern, called a *rotatory* gallop. Thus, there are four possible gallop patterns.

C-shaped gallop | Z-shaped gallop

large print–front feet
small print–rear feet

*Bounds* (also known as hops and jumps) are characterized by the synchronization of the hind feet; both strike the ground at the same time, side by side. The front feet strike the ground at a different time than the hind feet. In a full bound, the front feet are synchronized and strike the ground

full bound | half bound

side by side at the same time. In a half bound, only the hind feet are synchronized and the front feet hit the ground staggered. Animals that mostly use full bounds, also called hops, live in trees (tree squirrels and songbirds), whereas those that mostly use half bounds live on the ground (ground squirrels, rabbits, and grouse).

In a *pronk* (also called a *stot*), all four feet strike the ground at the same time, with the front feet side by side and forward of the hind feet, which are also side by side. This gait is often used by deer to gain height and increase time in the air to look around.

pronk

To increase peripheral vision, nonprimate mammals have eyes placed toward the sides of their heads, not flat on their face like humans. By turning sideways, a prey species can see what is pursuing it and where it needs to go to escape. The predator, by turning sideways, can see what it is chasing and where the rest of the predator pack is.

Consequently, quadrupedal mammals have evolved to use all gaits while their body is turned to the side. These *side gaits* result when the animal's heavy head deviates from the line of travel and the body turns sideways. First, the front feet respond by moving toward the side of the trail where the head is. Then, as the head turns more, the hind feet move to the side away from the head. The greater the head movement, the greater the angle of the side gait. Common examples are the side trot and side gallop

slow side trot

side gallop

often used by canids. These are often called a dog trot or dog gallop.

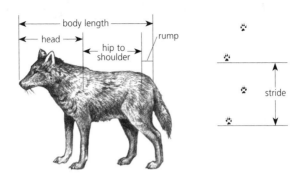

**estimating mammal length from stride**

An animal's size is also reflected in its gait patterns. When a mammal is walking with its normal gait, for example, the stride is 1.1 to 1.25 times longer than the distance from the hip to the shoulder joint. Using this crude relationship, body size can be judged from a walking stride. A 22-inch stride indicates a hip-to-shoulder length of 20 inches. Add to the hip-to-shoulder distance an estimate for the head length beyond the shoulder joint and an estimate of the rump length beyond the hip joint to get a total estimate of animal body length.

Speed also modifies gait patterns in trails. There are three rules governing how pattern changes as speed changes.

1. As speed increases, the hind foot lands farther forward than the front footprint on the same side. Conversely, as speed decreases, the hind foot lands farther back in relation to the front footprint.
2. As speed increases, stride increases.
3. As speed increases, straddle usually decreases.

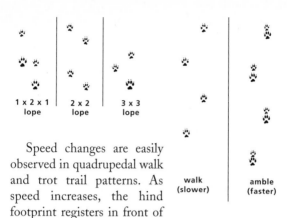

Speed changes are easily observed in quadrupedal walk and trot trail patterns. As speed increases, the hind footprint registers in front of the front print. This faster version of a walk is called an amble. The faster version of a trot doesn't have a name. When the animal slows to the point that the hind feet are registering behind the front prints, the animal may be stalking something. Trots are separated from walks by having a stride two or more times greater than the estimated hip-to-shoulder distance of an animal.

A slow version of the gallop is also recognizable. When a gallop slows to the point that one or more hind feet register behind the leading edge of the frontmost footprint in a group pattern, the gait is called a lope. The gait is still a gallop; it's just a slow gallop.

**Trail measurements**

The terms *stride, group, intergroup,* and *straddle* describe the size of an animal trail. The *stride* is measured from the point where a foot touches the ground surface to where the same point of the same foot next touches the surface, and consists of one group and one intergroup measurement. The *group* consists of all four footprints (two fronts, two hinds, two lefts, two rights), while the *intergroup* is the distance between groups. Gait patterns take their name from the configuration of the group. The stride provides an indication of size in a walking animal and an indication of relative speed for other gaits (see pages 15 and 16).

The *straddle* indicates the width of the trail and is measured from the outside rightmost pad of the outside right footprint of a group to the outside leftmost pad footprint of the same group. The outside edges of the trail are used because the insides of footprints overlap for many carnivore species. When measured from outside right to outside left, walking stride is an indicator of size.

Stride, group, and intergroup are all measured parallel to the trail, while the straddle is measured at right angles to the trail. Select a straight section of trail on level ground to measure. The slightest curve in the trail will distort the straddle measurement.

# Glossary of terms

**amble:** a fast walk in which the hind footprint registers anterior to the front footprint. See illustration on page 16.

**asymmetrical:** not symmetrical; that is, one side is not a mirror image of the opposite side.

**bound:** a gait in which both hind feet strike the ground at the same time, side by side. If the front feet also land side by side, the motion is said to be a full bound. A half bound occurs when one front foot strikes the ground in front of the other. See illustration on page 13.

**clout:** term used to refer to toe 3 or toe 4 of the hoof. See illustration on page 22.

**convergent toes:** toes 2 and 4 of ducks, geese, and swans, which bend toward the foot axis, especially at the tips. Compare to divergent toes.

**cord:** See *scat shape*.

**cough pellet:** remnants of bones and hair coughed up by many bird species after feeding on prey.

**dewclaw:** toe that over evolutionary time has become reduced in size and raised on the leg, away from the other toes; for example, toe 1 in dogs and toes 2 and 5 in deer.

**diagnostic:** providing certain identification of an animal or its sign.

**digit:** one of the toes of an animal.

**digital pad:** See *pad*.

**digitigrade:** walking on the tips of the toes. Dogs and cats, for example, are digitigrade. Tracks left by digitigrade animals rarely show a sole. Compare to *plantigrade*.

**distal webbing:** See *webbing*.

**divergent toes:** toes that are straight or turn out from the foot axis at the tips, specifically toes 2 and 4 of seagulls. Compare to convergent toes.

**foot axis:** imaginary line down the center of the foot. It runs between toes 3 and 4 in deer and their relatives, and down toe 3 of other mammals. In birds, the foot axis also runs down toe 3.

**fringe:** webbing attached to a single toe. May have a smooth edge, known as a simple fringe

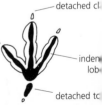

detached cl

inden
lob

detached tc

or simple lobe, or it may be wavy, in which case it is said to have indented lobes.

**full bound:** See *bound*.

**gait:** term for the type(s) of movement an animal uses when moving. Examples of gaits include walk, amble, trot, bound, and gallop. Gaits are defined by the mechanics of body movement, not by speed.

**gallop:** a gait in which hind feet move around the front feet and (usually) strike the ground in front of the front feet. Galloping forms distinct group patterns (two fronts, two hinds, two lefts, two rights) separated by an intergroup distance from the next set of four feet. Gallops fall into two basic patterns: Z-shaped and C-shaped.

**group:** a subunit of a stride including four footprints (two fronts and two hinds, and two lefts and two rights). The measure of the group plus the intergroup equals the measure of the stride.

**half bound:** See *bound*.

**heel:** portion of foot or track to the rear of digital and interdigital pads. In mammals, may be covered with hair, naked (without hair), or have one or more proximal pads. In reptiles and amphibians, may be textured with tubercles.

gallops          bounds

**hop:** synonymous with bound; often used in reference to gaits of rodents and rabbits.

**indented lobe:** See *fringe*.

**interdigital pad:** See *pad*.

**length:** of a track, the distance from front of toe pads to back of the interdigital pads, measured parallel to the foot axis. In mammal tracks, does not include claws. In bird tracks, does not include toe 1, but includes claws if they are attached and indistinguishable from toe pad.

**line of travel:** imaginary line on the ground over which the center of gravity of an animal passes.

**lobe:** See *fringe*.

**lope:** a slow gallop, in which at least one hind foot registers behind a front foot in a group of four footprints. See illustration on page 16.

**mesial webbing:** See *webbing*.

**minimum outline:** See pages 10 and 11 for extended discussion.

**nipple-dimple:** See *scat shape*.

**outer toe angle:** in birds, the angle between toes 2 and 4. In perching birds less than 90 degrees and in shorebirds greater than 120 degrees.

**oval:** See *scat shape*.

**pad:** hard, calluslike structure on the sole of an animal's foot. Each toe may have a digital pad. One or more interdigital pads are located directly to the rear of the toes, and one or more proximal pads may be located directly to the rear of the interdigital pads. In deer and their relatives, there is a single pad separated from the wall by the subunguinis. In birds, a metatarsal pad may occur directly under the leg bone.

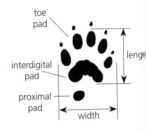

**plantigrade:** walking on the soles of the foot. Raccoons, bears, and humans, for example, are plantigrade. The sole of the foot usually shows in the footprint. Compare to *digitigrade*.

**pronk:** a gait in which all four feet strike the ground simultaneously and directly below the body. The group pattern shows two front footprints ahead of the two hind prints. Also called a stot. See illustration on page 14.

**proximal pad:** See *pad*.

**proximal webbing:** See *webbing*.

**rotatory gallop:** a type of gallop that tends to form a C-shaped group pattern. See illustration on page 13.

**run:** a gait used when moving only on two legs. It differs from a walk in having a longer stride.

**scat shape:** Cords are long pieces of scat, typically four to ten times longer than the width. Ends may be blunt or tapered. Ovals are pieces of scat typically two to four times longer than wide and tapered at both ends. A nipple-dimple shaped scat pellet has a point at one end and a depression at the other. See chart on page 9.

**simple fringe, simple lobe:** See *fringe*.

**sole:** bottom of an animal's foot. It may be covered with hair or naked, and may have one or more pads on it.

**stot:** See *pronk*.

**straddle:** the distance from the right edge of the rightmost pad to the leftmost edge of the leftmost pad in a trail. Measured at right angles to the line of travel.

**stot** **stride:** the distance from the point where a foot touches the ground to the point where the same foot touches the ground again. Measured parallel to the line of travel. One stride is equal to a group plus an intergroup measurement.

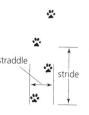

**subunguinis:** the soft material under the nails of humans. In deer and their relatives, refers specifically to the soft material between the pad and wall.

**symmetrical:** having two sides, one the mirror image of the other side.

**toe pad:** See *pad*.

**track**: refers to an individual footprint. Some measurable characteristics include length and width.

**track pattern:** the gross visual image of the pattern of footprints on the ground. A repeating pattern of two prints separated from the next two is called two-by and written 2 x 2. Prints may also show patterns of 3 x 3, 4 x 4, and 1 x 2 x 1. These patterns are made during a gallop or a bound. A few of these patterns are illustrated on pages 12 to 14.

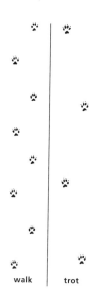

**trail:** a series of footprints and associated sign that marks the passage of an animal. Some measurable characteristics include stride and straddle.

**transverse gallop:** a type of gallop that tends to form a Z-shaped group pattern. See illustration on page 13.

**trot:** a gait in which evenly spaced footprints alternate on right and left sides of the line of travel. Hind footprint registers on top of front. As speed increases, hind moves forward of front. Same patterns as a walk, but longer stride. May be done with body turned to side. See illustration on page 14.

**walk**     **trot**

**tubercle:** rough pinhead-size protuberance on the sole of the foot of a reptile or amphibian.

**unguinis:** hard material forming nails in humans, hoof walls in deer and their relatives, and claws in other mammals. Composed of hair pasted together by body glues.

**walk:** a gait where evenly spaced footprints alternate on right and left sides of the line of travel. Hind footprint registers on top of front. As speed increases, hind moves forward of front. See illustrations on pages 12 and 16.

**wall:** hard material around the edge of each clout of a hoof. Technically the unguinis, which also forms human nails and animal claws.

**webbing:** thin membrane stretched between toes of animals. The webbing may be near the tips of the toes (distal), about midway to the toe tips (mesial), or attached at the base (proximal). A membrane attached to only one toe is called a fringe.

**width:** of a track, the greatest distance from the right side of the pads of a foot to the left side, whether the greatest distance is across the toes or palm pads. Measured perpendicular to the foot axis. In bird tracks, includes claws if they are attached and indistinguishable from toe pad.

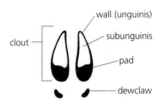

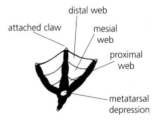

# How to use *Scats and Tracks*

*Scats and Tracks of North America* is designed for easy use in the field. The gray bars found on the edges of the pages of the track accounts will help you measure scat diameter and footprint size; each of these bars is keyed to the average size of the sign in question. A ruler is provided on the back cover. Below, I provide the background knowledge that every tracker should be familiar with before going to the field or using this book. Please take some time to study this material.

## Illustrations

Illustrator Todd Telander applied his great ability to our collections of plaster casts, photographs, and slides, drawing on our experience to produce the most up-to-date and accurate illustrations possible. These drawings—made from the best specimens in a collection of thousands—represent the culmination of decades of tracking experience and are far more accurate than the tracker usually finds in tracking books. The tracks you find on the ground may not have as much detail or be as clear, but it is better to have an excellent drawing to compare to an imperfect track than to have to compare a track to a drawing lacking critical details.

## How to use the track accounts

The track accounts in this guide have been grouped by similar footprint characteristics. Each track account represents a single species or a group of species with similar track characteristics. Each account is presented across a two-page spread and is conveniently divided into sections as discussed below. A brief listing of visual characteristics used to identify an animal begins each track account, appearing beneath the common and scientific names of the species. These descriptions are general, and great variability of pattern can exist among animals in the field. I recommend consulting appropriate field identification guides.

**Track:** A concise description of key points of footprints, to be used for identification. The accompanying track illustrations are not at actual size, but, unless otherwise noted, actual (average) length of the footprint is shown as a bar on the right side of the right-hand page. Average width is shown as a bar on the bottom of the right-hand page. In the field, place the appropriate measurement bar next to the track to compare size. To take a numerical measurement, use the ruler printed on the back cover of the book.

The tracks illustrated are all from right feet, except in the entries for birds, where both feet are pictured. Numerical measurements are given in the form length x width. Note that measurements of mammal tracks do not include claws, that measurements of bird tracks include claws but do not include toe 1, and that measurements generally do not include parts of the foot that often do not register in a given species's track (e.g., heels in the hind feet of some rodent species).

**Trail:** The average size of the stride of the most commonly used gait or gaits is given. Other common or characteristic gaits, if any, are discussed. See track pattern in the Glossary of Terms on page 21. For more information on gaits in tracking, see my *Field Guide to Mammal Tracking in North America* (1986). Gaits are displayed up the right side of the right-hand page. If the common gait is a walk or trot, however, it may not be illustrated, since all walking and trotting patterns consist of right-left alternating patterns.

**Scat:** A description of scat supplements the drawing. Average scat width is shown as a bar up the side of the left-hand page. In the field, place the appropriate measurement bar next to the scat to compare sizes. To take a numerical measurement, use the ruler printed on the back cover of the book. Numerical measurements of scat are given under the illustrations in the form length x width. In cases of small scat, only width is given; thus, a single measurement always indicates diameter.

**Habitat:** To aid in locating and differentiating tracks, the animal's habitat preferences are listed. Some animals with large ranges, such as the beaver, are only found in specific habitats.

**Similar species:** Clues are provided to help differentiate an animal's tracks from similar tracks of other species. With these clues, identification should be possible.

**Other sign:** Other sign of animals, besides tracks and scat, are listed or illustrated to help with identification, and simply to provide more information on animal lives.

In addition, a distribution map is provided with each account. This gives a generalized picture of where in North America an animal may be found. Animals may move outside their common range. Animals that require specific habitats will of course not be evenly distributed through the shown range.

To make the best use of this guide, carry it with you into the field. When you come across an unfamiliar track or trail, open the book to the appropriate track account and place the page alongside the track for immediate on-site comparison.

# Visual key to tracks

This simple key includes birds, reptiles, amphibians, and mammals. It is arranged by the number of toes that show in a good footprint, ranging from no toes to two toes to five toes. Those animals that show four toes in the front print and five toes in the hind are listed between four- and five-toed animals.

---

### Fiddler and Horseshoe Crabs (pp. 30–33)

Two to several parallel series of holes in the ground. Trail may be 1 to 12 inches (2.5 to 30 cm) wide and include shell drag marks.

---

### Snakes (pp. 66–67)

Series of side-to-side trail undulations.

---

### Deer and Relatives (pp. 296–321)

Two toes form hard, cloven hoof. Dewclaws may show in deep print.

---

### Birds with Webbed Feet (pp. 70–89, 118–123)

Three toes facing forward, often a fourth toe facing backward. Claws may be detached from toes. Webbing between two or more toes.

---

### Birds without Webbed Feet (pp. 90–117, 124–141)

Three toes facing forward, often a fourth toe facing backward. Claws may be detached from toes.

---

### Foxes, Coyotes, and Wolves (pp. 148–159)

Four toes in front and hind prints. Claws usually present and detached. Single anterior lobe on interdigital pad.

### Mountain Lions, Cats, and Relatives (pp. 160–171)

Four toes in front and hind prints. Claws usually absent. Double anterior lobe on interdigital pad.

### Armadillo (pp. 146–147)

Four toes in front print and five toes in hind. Often only the prominent inner toes—two on front, three on hind—register.

### Rabbits and Relatives (pp. 206–221)

Four toes in front and hind footprint. An exceptionally clear print may show a fifth inner toe in the front footprint. Pads lacking, bottom of foot covered with hair. Long hopping heel in hind print.

### Salamanders (pp. 34–39)

Four toes in front print, five toes in hind. Trail wide, often with a tail drag.

### Frogs (pp. 44–51)

Four toes in front print, five toes in hind. Long, slender toes. Front print faces center of trail. Webbing in hind prints may be distal (at tips) or proximal (near base of toes).

### Toads (pp. 40–43)

Four toes in front print, five toes in hind. Front print faces center of trail. Mesial (middle of toe) webbing in hind print. Tubercles may show on front and hind prints.

### American Alligator (pp. 68–69)

Five toes on front foot. Inside and outside toes are opposite and form a straight line. Four toes on hind foot with a well-developed heel. Claws detached.

### Rodents (pp. 222–295)

Most have four toes in front prints and five in hind. Beaver has five toes in front print. Front toes show a 1-2-1 grouping; hind show a 1-3-1 grouping. Long hopping heel in hind print.

### Lizards (pp. 52–59)

Five toes in front and hind prints. Toes long and slender. Claws may be detached. Tail drag often present in trail.

### Turtles (pp. 60–65)

Five toes show in front tracks and four in hind tracks. Front prints toe in and hind prints may toe out. Feet are relatively broad. Claws robust and often visible. Sometimes the claws are the only visible signs on hard ground.

### Opossum (pp. 142–143)

Five toes. Distinct hind print with an opposable (like human thumb) inside toe protruding sideways from other toes. Outside toe is slightly separated from middle three toes.

### Shrews (pp. 144–145)

Five slender toes present on front and hind feet. In clear prints, four interdigital and two proximal pads may be seen.

### Ringtails, Coaties, and Raccoons (pp. 184–185)

Five toes in front and hind prints. Toes most often round or bulbous at ends. May have long, slender toes.

### Weasels and Relatives (pp. 186–205)

Five toes in front and hind prints, though the little toe (on inside of foot) may not show. Toes in a 1-3-1 grouping. Interdigital pad is chevron-shaped. Plantigrade hind foot.

### Bears (pp. 172–179)

Five toes in front and hind prints, though the little toe (on inside of foot) may not show. Toes evenly spaced. Plantigrade hind foot.

# Scats
### and
# Tracks
### of

North America

# Fiddler Crabs
*Uca* species

Small crab (*Uca pugilator*
illustrated here) with
squarish shell that tapers
at back and lacks notch
on edge. Eye stalk longer
than space between eyes. Males
have one large claw and one
small claw, females two smaller
claws. Multiple species are found along most
of the eastern coast.

*Uca pugilator*

**Track:** Each foot creates a simple small hole, which in very wet sand may be slightly elongated.

**Trail:** Series of roundish holes in roughly parallel lines. Stride varies 0.1 to 0.3 inch (0.3 to 0.8 cm). Straddle varies 0.75 to 1.0 inch (1.8 to 2.5 cm). Because the crab moves sideways, its eight feet create four lines of holes, but as the crab turns, the number of lines increases up to eight lines.

**Scat:** Not known.

**hole in sand with tracks**

**Habitat:** Sand beaches to muddy beaches for similar species. Burrows in area between tide marks.

**Similar species:** Footprint holes of ghost crabs usually elongate and leave wider trails, about 4.0 inches (10.0 cm). Parallel rows of dotlike tracks separate fiddler trails from all other species.

**Other sign:** Domed entrances to burrows and balls of sand excavated from the burrow.

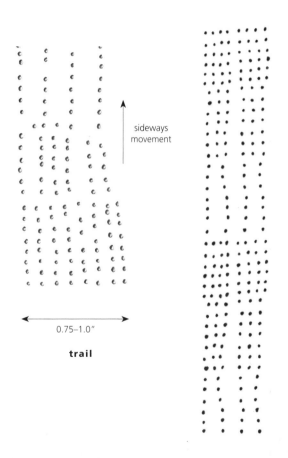

sideways movement

0.75–1.0"

**trail**

# Horseshoe Crab
*Limulus polyphemus*

Unmistakable hard
horseshoe-shaped shell
with tail spike. May reach
24.0 inches (61.0 cm) in length.
Not a crab but a relative of spiders.

**Track:** Walking footprints consisting of two elongate holes about 0.75 inch (1.9 cm) wide that form an inverted V. Rarely small hind feet register and look like ski pole baskets.

**Trail:** A wide, 10.0- to 12.0-inch (25.0- to 30.0-cm), drag mark through the sand consisting of two parallel rows of foot holes inside the shell drag mark. Distance between holes about 2.0 inches (5.0 cm). Tail drags down the middle of the trail.

**Scat:** Not known.

**egg mass on sandy beach**

**Habitat:** Intertidal to subtidal zones.

**Similar species:** Broad trail with footprint and tail drag is distinctive from other species.

**Other sign:** Series of round nest mounds where round, green eggs are deposited. Eggs occasionally exposed by water.

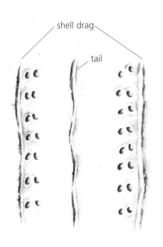

**tracks**
0.25 x 0.75 in
0.6 x 1.9 cm

# Eastern Newt—Red Eft phase
*Notophthalmus viridescens*

Vienna sausage–size salamander, up to 4.0 inches (10.0 cm) long. Moist, smooth skin. Terrestrial form, called red eft, is bright orange-red, with red spots outlined in black. Tubercles on underside of foot.

**Track:** Four toes on front foot (often only three show), and five toes on hind foot. The outline of the foot may not show, just toe prints. Even in a clear print, tubercles rarely show.

**Trail:** Walking stride is about 1.0 inch (2.5 cm). Trail has a wide straddle (0.67 inch/1.6 cm) relative to stride, and may show oscillating belly and tail drag marks.

**Scat:** Brown to black, with slightly tapered ends.

**Habitat:** Quiet waters around lakes, ponds, and streams in grassland meadow areas and forests.

**scat**
0.2 x 0.1 in
0.5 x 0.3 cm

SCAT WIDTH

**Similar species:** Differs from lizards by wider, oscillating tail drag (if present) and by having only four toes on front foot. Considerably smaller tracks and trail than most salamanders.

**Other sign:** Egg mass found in water along shore.

**front**
0.2 x 0.2 in
0.5 x 0.5 cm

**hind**
0.2 x 0.1 in
0.5 x 0.3 cm

**slow walk**

*FRONT TRACK LENGTH*

*FRONT TRACK WIDTH*

# Tiger Salamander
*Ambystoma tigrinum*

Hot dog–size
salamander, up to
9.0 inches (23.0
cm) long. Moist,
smooth skin. Body
brown to black to dark
green, with yellow spots
or streaks. Tubercles on underside of foot.

**Track:** Four toes on front foot (often only three show) and five toes on hind foot. The outline of the foot may not show, just toe prints. Even in a clear print, tubercles rarely show.

**Trail:** Walking stride is about 3.0 inches (7.5 cm). Trail has a wide straddle relative to stride and may show oscillating belly and tail drag marks.

**Scat:** Soft, pea-size black masses, with some hint of oval shape.

**scat**
0.3 x 0.2 in
0.8 x 0.5 cm

**egg mass**

SCAT WIDTH

**Habitat:** Quiet waters around lakes, ponds, and streams in grassland meadow areas and forests.

**Similar species:** Differs from lizards by wider, oscillating tail drag and by having only four toes on front foot. Larger tracks and trail than newts.

**Other sign:** Eggs in egg masses are attached individually to underwater plant stems.

**front**
0.6 x 0.3 in
1.5 x 0.8 cm

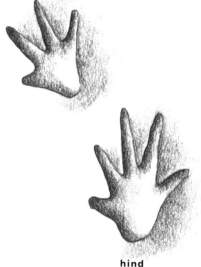

**hind**
0.8 x 0.6 in
2.0 x 1.5 cm

**slow walk**

FRONT TRACK LENGTH

FRONT TRACK WIDTH

# Spotted Salamander
*Ambystoma maculatum*

Hot dog–size
salamander, up
to 8.0 inches
(20.0 cm) long. Moist,
smooth skin. Body
black to bluish black, with two rows of yellow spots.
Tubercles on underside of foot.

**Track:** Four toes on front foot (often only three show) and five toes on hind foot. The outline of the foot may not show, just toe prints. Even in a clear print, tubercles rarely show.

**Trail:** Walking stride is about 3.0 inches (7.5 cm). Trail has a wide straddle relative to stride and may show oscillating belly and tail drag marks.

**Scat:** Soft, pea-size black masses, with some hint of oval shape.

**scat**
0.3 x 0.4 in
0.7 x 0.6 cm

**egg mass**

**Habitat:** Quiet waters around lakes, ponds, and streams in grassland meadow areas and mixed deciduous forests. Under stones, logs, and boards during wet weather.

**Similar species:** Differs from lizards by wider, oscillating tail drag and by having only four toes on front foot. Larger tracks and trail than newts.

**Other sign:** Eggs in egg masses may be attached to underwater plant stems.

**front**
0.6 x 0.3 in
1.5 x 0.8 cm

**hind**
0.8 x 0.6 in
2.0 x 1.5 cm

**slow walk**

*FRONT TRACK LENGTH*

*FRONT TRACK WIDTH*

# Boreal Toad
*Bufo boreas*

Baseball-size toad, up to 3.5 inches (9.0 cm) long. Body is plain brown to gray to reddish, with warts from yellow to red in dark brown or black spots. A white line runs down the back. Only one or two large warts in each dark spot. Female larger than male. Found in western North America. The American toad (*B. americanus*) of the eastern half of North America is similar in size; tracks and sign are similar.

**Track:** Four toes on front foot and five on hind. Front feet face in. Two tubercles on heel of front foot. Three hind toes face in, one forward, and one out. Two tubercles may show on the heel of the hind foot and can be confused with toes. Webbing, found only on hind feet, extends at most halfway out to toe tips.

**Trail:** Hopping or full bound stride generally 5.0 to 7.0 inches (13.0 to 18.0 cm). Walking stride is about 2.5 inches (6.3 cm).

**scat**
0.9 x 0.2 in
2.3 x 0.5 cm

**egg mass**

**toad imprint in mud**

SCAT WIDTH

**Scat:** Dark brown to black. Long cord, up to five times longer than wide. Sometimes contains insect parts.

**Habitat:** Lakes, ponds, beaver ponds, and wet mixed coniferous forest.

**Similar species:** Differs from frog by presence of tubercles on front heels. Hind foot is narrower than frog. Walks and uses short hops more than the usually long-hopping frog.

**Other sign:** Long strings of egg masses on bottom of water source and floating among vegetation.

**walk**

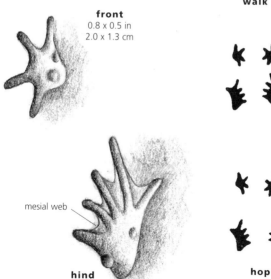

**front**
0.8 x 0.5 in
2.0 x 1.3 cm

mesial web

**hind**
1.0 x 0.9 in
2.5 x 2.3 cm

**hop**

*FRONT TRACK LENGTH*

*FRONT TRACK WIDTH*

# Woodhouse's Toad
*Bufo woodhousei*

**Baseball-size toad, up to 5.0 inches (12.5 cm) long. Body is light brown to gray to green, with warty skin and dark spots. A white line runs down the back. Female larger than male.**

**Track:** Four toes on front foot and five on hind. Front feet face in. Tubercles on heel of front foot. Four hind toes face in, one faces out. Two tubercles may show on the heel of the hind foot and can be confused with toes. Webbing, found only on hind feet, extends at most halfway out to toe tips.

**Trail:** Walking stride is about 3.0 inches (7.5 cm). Hopping stride generally less than 1.0 foot (0.3 m).

**scat**
1.0 x 0.3 in
2.5 x 0.8 cm

**egg mass**

**toad imprint in mud**

SCAT WIDTH

**Scat:** Dark brown to black. Long cord, up to five times longer than wide. Sometimes contains insect parts.

**Habitat:** Lakes, ponds, beaver ponds.

**Similar species:** Differs from frogs by presence of tubercles on front heels. Hind foot is narrower than frog. Walks and uses short hops more than the usually long-hopping frog.

**Other sign:** Long strings of egg masses on pond and lake bottoms and floating among vegetation.

**walk**

**front**
0.9 x 0.6 in
2.3 x 1.5 cm

mesial web

**hind**
1.1 x 0.9 in
2.8 x 2.3 cm

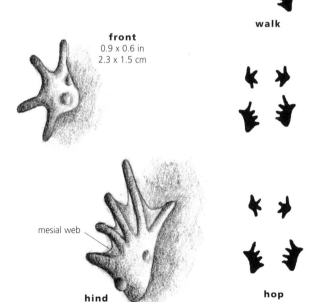

**hop**

FRONT TRACK LENGTH

FRONT TRACK WIDTH

# Chorus Frog
*Pseudacris triseriata*

**Silver dollar–size frog, less than 1.5 inches (3.8 cm). Highly variable frog, with body color from brown to green. Darker stripe pattern varies with subspecies.**

**Track:** Four toes on front foot and five on hind. Front feet face in. Four hind toes face in, one faces out. Proximal webbing on hind feet extending at most one-quarter of way out to toe tips.

**Trail:** Hopping stride about 10.0 inches (25.0 cm). Frogs may easily hop 3.0 feet (1.0 m) when in a hurry.

**scat**
0.5 x 0.1 in
1.3 x 0.3 cm

**egg mass and tadpole**

SCAT WIDTH

**Scat:** Black, firm cord with slightly tapering ends.

**Habitat:** Shallow water with emergent vegetation, including pond and lake shores, marshes, and beaver ponds.

**Similar species:** Lacks the palm tubercles of the front feet of toad. Less webbing between toes. Hops more and longer distances. Smaller than leopard frog.

**Other sign:** Inconspicuous egg masses consisting of a few eggs in a packet attached to vegetation below waterline.

**walk**

**hop**

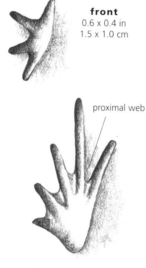

**front**
0.6 x 0.4 in
1.5 x 1.0 cm

proximal web

**hind**
0.8 x 0.6 in
2.0 x 1.5 cm

FRONT TRACK LENGTH

FRONT TRACK WIDTH

# Spotted Frog
*Rana pretiosa*

Baseball-size frog, 3.8 inches (9.5 cm) long. Body light to dark brown, with spots. Spots have light-colored centers. White stripe from jaw to shoulder. Salmon color on lower half of belly.

**Track:** Four toes on front foot and five on hind. Front feet face in. Four hind toes face in, one faces out. Webbing, found only on hind feet, is distal, extending most of the way out to toe tips. Toe 1 is thick on male because it serves as the nuptial pad for grasping female during mating.

**Trail:** Hopping stride is about 20.0 inches (50.0 cm). May easily hop 3.0 feet (1.0 m) when in a hurry.

**Scat:** Brown to black, with slightly tapered ends.

**Habitat:** Cold, nonseasonal ponds, streams, and other water sources. Not found in ponds overgrown with cattails.

**scat**
1.5 x 0.4 in
3.8 x 1.0 cm

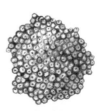

**egg mass**

SCAT WIDTH

**Similar species:** Nuptial pad (enlarged pad for holding female during mating) separates male from other hopping amphibians. Differs from toads by more webbing between toes, lack of palm tubercles on front feet, and by hopping more and at longer distances. Larger than boreal chorus frog.

**Other sign:** Softball-size egg masses floating just below water surface.

**front**
0.8 x 0.5 in
2.0 x 1.3 cm

**walk**

distal web

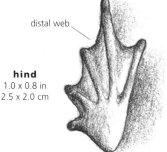

**hind**
1.0 x 0.8 in
2.5 x 2.0 cm

**hop**

FRONT TRACK LENGTH

FRONT TRACK WIDTH

# Leopard Frog

*Rana pipiens* (northern) and
*R. utricularia* (southern)

**Baseball-size frog, up to
3.5 inches (8.8 cm). Body
light to dark brown or
green, with dark spots.
Spots have light borders.
White stripe on jaw.**

**Track:** Four toes on front foot and five on hind. Front feet face in. Four hind toes face in, one faces out. Webbing, found only on hind feet, is distal, extending most of the way out to toe tips. Toe 1 is thick on male because it serves as the nuptial pad for grasping female during mating.

**Trail:** Full bound or hopping stride is about 20.0 inches (50.0 cm). May easily hop 3.0 feet (1.0 m) when in a hurry. Occasionally walk.

**Scat:** Brown to black, with slightly tapered ends.

**Habitat:** Cold, nonseasonal ponds, streams, and other water sources. May be found in meadows well away from water.

**scat**
1.5 x 0.4 in
3.8 x 1.0 cm

**egg mass**

**Similar species:** Nuptial pad (enlarged pad for holding female during mating) separates male from other hopping amphibians. Differs from toads by more webbing between toes, lack of palm tubercles on front feet, and by hopping more and at longer distances. Differs from bullfrog by larger feet. Larger than chorus frog.

**Other sign:** Softball-size egg masses floating just below water surface.

**walk**

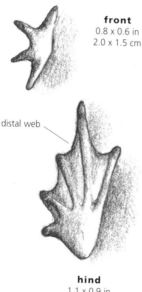

**front**
0.8 x 0.6 in
2.0 x 1.5 cm

distal web

**hind**
1.1 x 0.9 in
2.8 x 2.3 cm

**hop**

FRONT TRACK LENGTH

FRONT TRACK WIDTH

# Bullfrog
*Rana catesbeiana*

Softball-size frog, 4.0 to 8.0 inches (10.0 to 20.0 cm). Brownish green to green, becoming light green on head. Legs banded with dark brown to green; small spots on back. Fold of skin around eye and large exposed eardrum.

**Track:** Four toes on front foot and five on hind. Front feet face in. Three hind toes face in, remaining two face forward or out. Webbing, found only on hind feet, is distal, extending most of the way out to the toe tips. In a clear track, a male's toe 2 on front foot appears thicker at base.

**Trail:** Hopping stride is 24.0 inches (60.0 cm). May easily hop 72.0 inches (180.0 cm).

**scat**
1.5 x 0.4 in
3.8 x 1.0 cm

**Scat:** Brown to black, with slightly tapered ends.

**Habitat:** Permanent and (usually) quiet water with dense growth of aquatic plants, especially cattails, in plains, woodlands, and forest.

**Similar species:** Differs from toads by more webbing between toes, lack of palm tubercles on front feet, and by hopping more and at longer distances. Differs from leopard frog and chorus frog by larger feet.

**Other sign:** Deposits a globular egg mass.

**walk**

**front**
1.5 x 1.0 in
3.8 x 2.5 cm

distal web

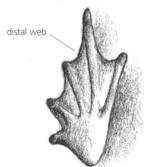

**hind**
1.8 x 0.9 in
4.5 x 2.3 cm

**hop**

FRONT TRACK LENGTH

FRONT TRACK WIDTH

# Prairie or Fence Lizard

*Sceloporus undulatus*

Roughly the size of a
roll of Life Savers; body
about 3.0 inches (7.5 cm),
with dry skin and ridged
scales. Gray to dark brown
above, with black crossbars
(southwestern plains) or longitudinal stripes (southeastern
plains). Considerable subspecies variation.

**Track:** Five relatively long, thin toes on front and hind feet. Hind heel is relatively long. Claws may show.

**Trail:** Trotting stride is about 3.0 inches (7.5 cm). Hind feet mostly register on top of front feet. Relatively wide straddle. Tail drag present.

**Scat:** Brown cord, six to eight times longer than wide. White nitrogenous material usually found on one end.

**Habitat:** Wide variety of habitats including forests, woodland, prairie, and rock outcrops. Shelters in bushes, trees, under rocks, or in logs.

**scat**
1.5 x 0.25 in
3.8 x 0.6 cm

**Similar species:** Differs from salamanders by having five narrow toes on front feet and straighter tail drag. Differs from horned lizard by narrower footprint.

**Other sign:** Scuff marks in dust may indicate a dust bath.

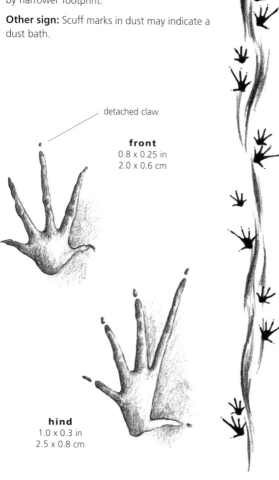

detached claw

**front**
0.8 x 0.25 in
2.0 x 0.6 cm

**hind**
1.0 x 0.3 in
2.5 x 0.8 cm

**slow walk**

FRONT TRACK LENGTH

FRONT TRACK WIDTH

# Sagebrush Lizard
*Sceloporus graciosus*

Roughly the size of a roll of Life Savers; body less than 2.5 inches (6.3 cm), with dry skin and ridged, spiny scales. Gray to brown, with light stripes running length of body. White to light tan belly. Male has bright blue patches on each side of belly and under throat. Female has light blue in same region and salmon color between legs.

**Track:** Five relatively long, thin toes on front and hind feet. Hind heel is relatively long. Claws may show.

**Trail:** Running stride is about 3.0 inches (7.5 cm). Hind feet mostly register on top of front feet. Relatively wide straddle. Tail drag present.

**Scat:** Brown cord, six to eight times longer than wide. White nitrogenous material usually found on one end.

**scat**
1.5 x 0.25 in
3.8 x 0.6 cm

**Habitat:** South-facing slopes; warm, open, rocky areas; and forest edges having downed logs.

**Similar species:** Differs from salamanders by having five narrow toes on front feet and straight trail drag.

**Other sign:** Scuff marks in dust may indicate a dust bath.

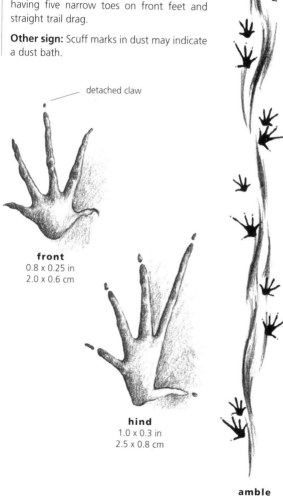

detached claw

**front**
0.8 x 0.25 in
2.0 x 0.6 cm

**hind**
1.0 x 0.3 in
2.5 x 0.8 cm

**amble**

FRONT TRACK LENGTH

FRONT TRACK WIDTH

# Short-horned Lizard
*Phrynosoma douglassi*

Roughly the size of a calling
card; body and tail
less than 4.0 inches
(10.0 cm) long. Body
relatively broad, with
short horns projecting from
back of head. A single row of
fringe scales along edge of body.
Body mottled gray to brown to tan, closely matching local
terrain colors.

**Track:** Five relatively long, thin toes on front and hind feet. Hind heel is relatively long. Claws may show.

**Trail:** Trotting stride is 3.0 inches (7.5 cm). Hind feet mostly register on top of front feet. Relatively wide straddle. Relatively straight tail drag and often a wider body drag.

**Scat:** Brown pellets three to six times longer than wide; may be tapered. White nitrogenous material may be found on one end.

**scat**
1.5 x 0.25 in
3.8 x 0.6 cm

SCAT WIDTH

**Habitat:** Determined by presence of fine, loose soil interspersed with firm, sandy or rocky terrain. Found in prairies and open woodlands, from plains high into mountains.

**Similar species:** Differs from salamanders by having five narrow toes on front feet and relatively straight tail drag.

**Other sign:** Scuff marks in loose sand where the lizard buries itself for camouflage.

detached claw

**front**
about 0.8 x 0.6 in
about 2.0 x 1.5 cm

**hind**
about 1.0 x 0.6 in
about 2.5 x 1.5 cm

**trot**

*FRONT TRACK LENGTH*

*FRONT TRACK WIDTH*

# Texas Horned Lizard
*Phrynosoma cornutum*

Roughly the size of a calling card; body and tail less than 4.0 inches (10.0 cm) long. Body relatively broad, with horns projecting from back of head. Central two head spines are much longer than others. Body mottled gray to brown to tan, closely matching local terrain colors. Two rows of fringe scales along edge of body.

**Track:** Five relatively long, thin toes on front and hind feet. Hind heel is relatively long. Claws may show.

**Trail:** Trotting stride is 3.0 inches (7.5 cm). Hind feet mostly register on top of front feet. Relatively wide straddle. Relatively straight tail drag and often a wider body drag.

**Scat:** Brown pellets three to six times longer than wide; may be tapered. White nitrogenous material may be found on one end.

**scat**
1.5 x 0.25 in
3.8 x 0.6 cm

**Habitat:** Determined by presence of fine, loose soil interspersed with firm, sandy or rocky terrain. Found in prairies and open woodlands, from plains high into mountains.

**Similar species:** Differs from salamanders by having five narrow toes on front feet and relatively straight tail drag. Differs from fence lizard by wider footprint.

**Other sign:** Scuff marks in loose sand where the lizard buries itself for camouflage.

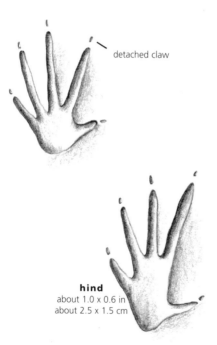

**front**
about 0.8 x 0.6 in
about 2.0 x 1.5 cm

detached claw

**hind**
about 1.0 x 0.6 in
about 2.5 x 1.5 cm

**trot**

FRONT TRACK LENGTH

FRONT TRACK WIDTH

# Snapping Turtle
*Chelydra serpentina*

Large to very large turtle, average 10.0 to 30.0 pounds (4.5 to 14.0 kg). The robust shell is lined by three toothed ridges. Large head with robust, hooked jaw. Tail longer than half the shell and toothed on top.

**Track:** Five toes show in front tracks and four in hind tracks. Front prints toe in and hind prints may toe out. Feet are relatively broad. Claws robust and often visible. Sometimes the claws are the only visible sign on hard ground.

**Trail:** Walking stride ranges 5.0 to 12.0 inches (12.5 to 30.0 cm). Straddle is wide compared to stride. Tail drag often present.

**Scat:** Lacks well-defined shape. Color is algae-green to dark black. Often soft.

**scat**
1.5 in
3.8 cm

SCAT WIDTH

**Habitat:** Always near water, including swamps, marshes, lakes, streams, and rivers.

**Similar species:** Broad trail of five-toed, clawed track with a tail drag separates the snapping turtle track and trail.

**Other sign:** Nest in open area where sun warms sand and eggs. Nest may be several inches deep.

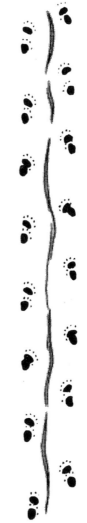

**front**
1.6 x 2.0 in
4.0 x 5.0 cm

**hind**
3.2 x 2.6 in
8.0 x 6.4 cm

**slow walk**

FRONT TRACK LENGTH

FRONT TRACK WIDTH

# Atlantic Loggerhead Turtle
*Caretta caretta*

**Very large sea
turtle, 170.0 to
350.0 pounds
(80.0 to 160.0 kg).
Reddish brown with five or
more coastal (side) plates.**

**Track:** Flipper-shaped limbs with
two claws leave two holes in the
sand. In hard sand, only the front end
of the flipper may show. Footprints
may be obliterated by the dragging
motion of front legs scraping the sand.
Hind feet often only a drag mark.

**Trail:** Walking stride about 12.0 inches
(30.0 cm). Straddle is wide compared
to stride, 28.0 to 36.0 inches (70.0 to
90.0 cm). Front feet, which sweep
backward and in, register well outside
the shell drag mark which is 8.0 to 12.0 inches (20.0 to 30.0 cm)
wide. Front feet may push up mounds of sand. Hind feet often
show only as drag marks.

**Scat:** Not known; turtle defecates in water.

**Habitat:** Ocean beaches.

**sand mound with flipper kick marks**

**Similar species:** Broad dragging trail of shell with parallel rows of two holes on each side of shell drag mark separates sea turtles from other turtles.

**Other sign:** Nests 12.0 inches (30.0 cm) deep are dug in beach sand.

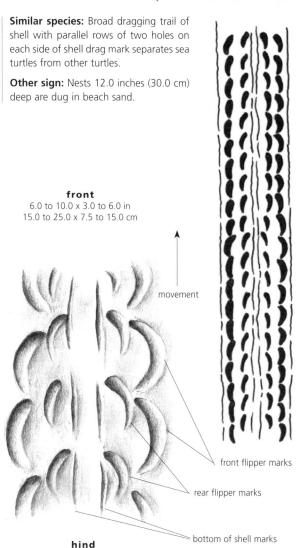

**front**
6.0 to 10.0 x 3.0 to 6.0 in
15.0 to 25.0 x 7.5 to 15.0 cm

movement

front flipper marks

rear flipper marks

bottom of shell marks

**hind**
6.0 to 8.0 x 5.0 to 7.0 in
15.0 to 20.0 x 12.5 to 18.0 cm

FRONT TRACK LENGTH

FRONT TRACK WIDTH

# Painted Turtle
*Chrysemys picta*

Small turtle with
smooth, unkeeled
shells and patterns
of red, yellow, and
black. Length to 8.0
inches (20.0 cm). Female
larger than male.

**Track:** Five toes with claws show in front
prints. Claws longer on front feet; claws
of male's front feet are two to three times
longer than female's. Outer toe on hind
foot lacks claw. Distal webbing on front
and hind prints.

**Trail:** Walking stride averages 4.5 inches
(11.5 cm), with a straddle of 4.0 inches
(10.0 cm). Front feet toe in and hind feet toe out. Hind footprint
registers slightly behind. Tail drag often visible.

**Scat:** Usually black semiliquid, slightly elongated clumps.

**scat**
0.9 x 0.2 in
2.3 x 0.5 cm

SCAT WIDTH

**Habitat:** Ponds, lakes, marshes, swamps, streams, and ditches with abundant vegetation.

**Similar species:** Differs from snapping turtle by its narrow straight trail.

**Other sign:** Nests are usually dug in sand in open areas where sun warms eggs.

**front**
0.8 x 0.7 in without
claws
2.0 x 1.8 cm

**hind**
1.1 x 1.0 in without
claws
2.8 x 2.5 cm

**walk**

FRONT TRACK LENGTH

FRONT TRACK WIDTH

# Snakes
various species

A variety of
snakes, from garter
snakes (*Thamnophis sirtalis*)
to milk snakes (*Lampropeltis
triangulum*) to massaugas (*Sistrurus
catenatus*) to timber rattlesnakes
(*Crotalus viridis*).

**Rattlesnake**
*Crotalus viridis*

**Track:** No footprint to describe.

**Trail:** Varies from 1.0 to 4.0 inches (2.5 to 10.0 cm) wide. Characterized by side-to-side undulations of the trail. The period, the distance from one curve to the next, varies by species, age, and speed of the snake. Surface material is usually pushed up at the outside of each curve. Gait is either a side-to-side undulation or sidewinding.

**Scat:** Black or brown cord, with constrictions and undulations. White nitrogenous material often attached.

**scat**
4.0 x 0.4 in
10.0 x 1.0 cm

**shed skin**

**Habitat:** Varies widely—from water's edge to rock outcrops to dry sand dunes.

**Similar species:** Resembles no other track.

**Other sign:** Shed skin.

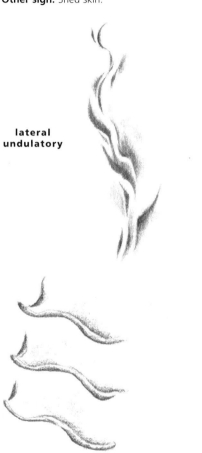

**lateral undulatory**

**sidewinding**

**trail**

# American Alligator
*Alligator mississippiensis*

**Adults range 6.0 to 12.0 feet (1.8 to 3.6 m). Body is black. Rounded snout.**

**Track:** Five toes on front foot. Inside and outside toes are opposite and form a straight line. Four toes on hind foot with a well-developed heel. Claws detached. Skin tubercles may show in the bottom of the tracks. Tracks size varies considerably because alligators grow their whole life.

**Trail:** Walking stride is about 40.0 inches (100.0 cm) but varies with alligator size.

**Scat:** I have not observed their scat.

**Habitat:** Prefers river swamps, marshes, and bayous.

**Similar species:** No similar tracks for adults. Young might be confused with turtles, but has four toes on hind feet.

**Other sign:** Nest composed of vegetation; may be up to 7.0 feet (2.1 m) in diameter and 3.0 feet (90.0 cm) high.

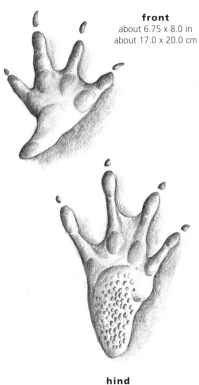

**front**
about 6.75 x 8.0 in
about 17.0 x 20.0 cm

**hind**
about 11.0 x 9.0 in
about 28.0 x 23.0 cm

**slow walk**

*FRONT TRACK LENGTH (50%)*

*FRONT TRACK WIDTH (50%)*

# Common Loon
*Gavia immer*

Large, long-bodied aquatic bird, average length 24.0 inches (60.0 cm). Dark-colored bird with black-and-white checkered back and neck band. Dark greenish head.

**Track:** Three toes showing, toes 2 to 4 pointing forward. Toe 1 does not register. Toes 2, 3, and 4 have claws and distal webbing.

**Trail:** Walking stride is 10.0 inches (25.0 cm) with a 7.0-inch (18.0-cm) straddle. Toes turn inward. Foot drag marks usually evident because the loon's legs are placed far back on its body, making walking difficult and causing the loon to drag its feet.

**Scat:** I have not observed their scat.

**nest**

**Habitat:** Freshwater lakes and rivers; near shore on ocean.

**Similar species:** Differs from all other aquatic birds by heavy drag marks in trail and relatively long, narrow feet.

**Other sign:** Large nest on reeds and brush at edge of water. Eggs appear large in small nest.

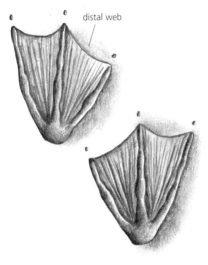

distal web

**feet**
5.25 x 4.3 in
13.1 x 10.8 cm

**walk**

*TRACK LENGTH*

*TRACK WIDTH (50%)*

# White Pelican
*Pelecanus erythrorhynchos*

Large aquatic bird, average length more
than 60.0 inches (150.0 cm),
with a wingspan of
more than 8.0 feet
(2.4 m). White
with black
primary wing
feathers. Large
bill is yellow to
orange.

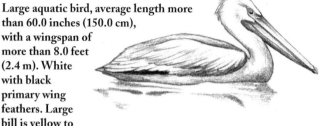

**Track:** Four long, slender toes. Toe 1
offset to side of track. Feet *totipalmate,*
with webbing between all four toes.
Webbing distal and slightly convex
between toes. Claws attached.

**Trail:** Walking stride averages 16.0
inches (40.0 cm). Toes turn inward.

**Scat:** Shapeless, brownish-white mass.

**Habitat:** Lakes, marshes, and bays. During summer found in
freshwater lakes; in winter found in salt water.

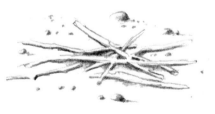

**ground nest**

**Similar species:** Differs from all other web-footed birds except cormorant by being toti-palmate. Differs from cormorant by having attached claws.

**Other sign:** Nests on ground in large island colonies.

distal web

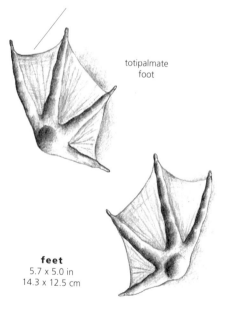

totipalmate
foot

**feet**
5.7 x 5.0 in
14.3 x 12.5 cm

**walk**

*TRACK LENGTH*

*TRACK WIDTH (50%)*

# Double-crested Cormorant
*Phalacrocorax auritus*

Large aquatic bird, average length more than 32.0 inches (80.0 cm), with a wingspan of more than 4.3 feet (1.3 cm). Dark body with orange throat patch. Crest of two white feathers behind eye, which may be difficult to see.

**Track:** Four long, slender toes. Toe 1 offset to side of track. Toe 4 is longest. Feet *totipalmate,* i.e., with webbing between all four toes. Webbing distal and slightly convex between toes. Claws detached.

**Trail:** Walking stride is about 10.0 inches (25.0 cm). Walks awkwardly on land, with a short stride for its size. Toes turn inward.

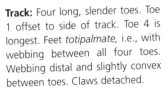

**ground nest**

**Scat:** Shapeless, nearly liquid white mass.

**Habitat:** Saltwater islands, bays, and cliffs. Freshwater lakes, ponds, and swamps.

**Similar species:** Differs from all other web-footed birds except pelican by being totipalmate. Differs from pelican by having detached claws.

**Other sign:** Nests in colonies on ground or in trees. Acidic scat kills trees and ground vegetation.

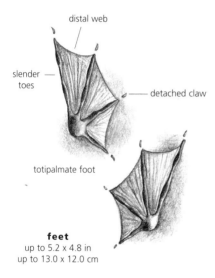

distal web

slender toes

detached claw

totipalmate foot

**feet**
up to 5.2 x 4.8 in
up to 13.0 x 12.0 cm

**walk**

TRACK LENGTH

*TRACK WIDTH (50%)*

# Green-backed Heron
*Butorides striatus*

Medium-size wading bird, average length 14.0 inches (36.0 cm). Male and female similar in overall appearance: blue to greenish body, with reddish-brown neck and yellowish legs.

**Track:** Four toes, toes 2 to 4 pointing forward. Small proximal web between toes 3 and 4. Footprint is asymmetrical, with toe 1 set to inside of foot axis (drawn through toe 3). On hard ground, metatarsal pad may not show (that is, toes may appear unconnected).

**Trail:** Walking stride about 10.0 inches (25.0 cm). Trail is fairly straight, and feet point forward.

**cough pellet**

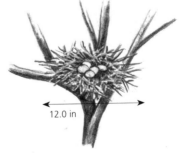

12.0 in

**nest**
4 to 5 eggs common

**Scat:** Semiliquid, predominantly white. Solid cords of scat vary from 1.0 to 3.0 inches (2.5 to 5.0 cm), and may contain fish, insects, frogs, and salamanders.

**Habitat:** Fresh- and saltwater areas along ponds, streams, lakes, swamps, and beaches where heavily wooded.

**Similar species:** Smaller version of great blue heron track (6.5 inches/16.5 cm). Differs from other shore-edge tracks by asymmetrical placement of toes.

**Other sign:** Undigested material may be coughed up as pellets.

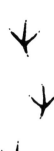

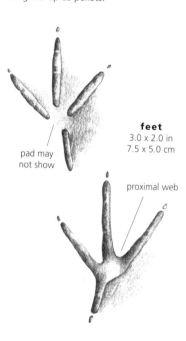

**feet**
3.0 x 2.0 in
7.5 x 5.0 cm

pad may
not show

proximal web

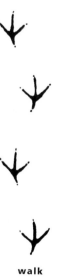

**walk**

*TRACK LENGTH*

*TRACK WIDTH*

# Great Blue Heron
*Ardea herodias*

Large wading bird, average length 45.0 inches (113.0 cm). Male and female similar in overall appearance: gray-blue body, with white neck and yellow beak. Black crown extends on feathers off rear of head.

**Track:** Four toes, toes 2 to 4 pointing forward. Small proximal web between toes 3 and 4. Footprint is asymmetrical, with toe 1 set to inside of foot axis (drawn through toe 3). Toe 1 is about 1.5 inches (3.8 cm); toe 2 is longer than 1, though shorter than 3 and 4. On hard ground, metatarsal pad may not show (that is, toes may appear unconnected).

**Trail:** Walking stride about 20.0 inches (50.0 cm). Trail is fairly straight and feet point forward.

**cough pellet**

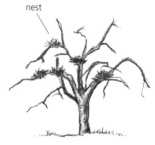

nest

**rookery**

**Scat:** Semiliquid, predominantly white. Solid cords of scat vary from 2.0 to 3.0 inches (5.0 to 7.5 cm) in length and may contain fish, frogs, salamanders, and even small rodents. Ground beneath nests becomes coated with droppings.

**Habitat:** Frequents backwater eddies along riverbanks and shallow edges of lakes.

**Similar species:** Differs from other shore-edge tracks by large size and asymmetrical placement of toes.

**Other sign:** Large colonies of nests high in trees. Undigested material may be coughed up as pellets.

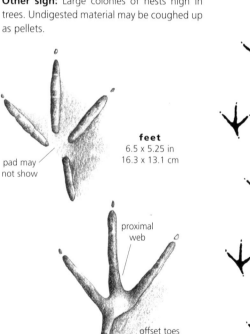

**feet**
6.5 x 5.25 in
16.3 x 13.1 cm

pad may not show

proximal web

offset toes

**walk**

TRACK LENGTH (50%)

TRACK WIDTH (50%)

# Trumpeter Swan
*Cygnus buccinator*

Large aquatic bird, length averaging 60.0 inches (150.0 cm). Male larger than female. Adult is all white, with a black beak. Immature swan has gray plumage. Male and female identically colored.

**Track:** Four toes. Toes 2 to 4, which point forward, usually register. Toe 1 points rearward and only occasionally shows. Distal webbing between toes 2, 3, and 4. Toes 2 and 4 tend to converge slightly near tips. Claws are broad, blunt, and attached to toes. Feet turned in.

**Trail:** Walking stride is about 14.0 inches (35.0 cm).

**Scat:** Cord, five to eight times longer than wide. Often greenish and coated with white nitrogenous deposits.

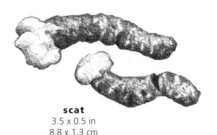

**scat**
3.5 x 0.5 in
8.8 x 1.3 cm

**Habitat:** Ponds, lakes, slowly flowing streams and rivers.

**Similar species:** Larger than ducks and geese. Differs from pelican and cormorant by lacking webbing between toes 1 and 2. Larger than gulls, also differing from them by having convergent toes and distal webbing.

**Other sign:** Nests on elevated areas, such as beaver lodges and muskrat houses, or on the ground. Eggs larger than eggs of Canada goose.

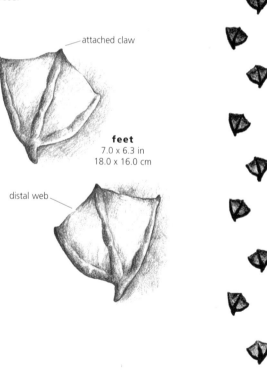

attached claw

**feet**
7.0 x 6.3 in
18.0 x 16.0 cm

distal web

**walk**

*TRACK LENGTH (50%)*

*TRACK WIDTH (50%)*

# Mute Swan
*Cygnus olor*

Large aquatic bird, length averaging 60.0 inches (150.0 cm). Male larger than female. Adult is all white, with an orange bill with a black knob at base. Immature swan has gray plumage. Male and female identically colored. Swims with curved neck and arched wings.

**Track:** Four toes. Toes 2 to 4, which point forward, usually register. Toe 1 points rearward and only occasionally shows. Distal webbing between toes 2, 3, and 4. Toes 2 and 4 tend to converge slightly near tips. Claws are broad, blunt, and attached to toes. Feet turned in.

**Trail:** Walking stride is about 14.0 inches (35.0 cm).

**Scat:** Cord, five to eight times longer than wide. Often greenish and coated with white nitrogenous deposits.

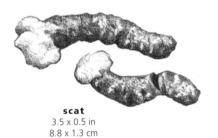

**scat**
3.5 x 0.5 in
8.8 x 1.3 cm

SCAT WIDTH

**Habitat:** Ponds, lakes, swamps, and slowly flowing streams and rivers, all with emergent vegetation.

**Similar species:** Larger than ducks and geese. Differs from pelican and cormorant by lacking webbing between toes 1 and 2. Larger than gulls, also differing from them by having convergent toes and distal webbing.

**Other sign:** Nests on elevated areas such as cattails, reeds, or roots. Eggs larger than eggs of Canada goose.

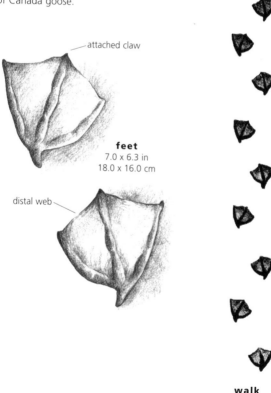

attached claw

**feet**
7.0 x 6.3 in
18.0 x 16.0 cm

distal web

**walk**

TRACK LENGTH (50%)

TRACK WIDTH (50%)

# Mallard Duck
*Anas platyrhynchos*

Aquatic bird with webbed feet, 20.0 to 26.0 inches (50.0 to 65.0 cm), 2.0 to 3.0 pounds (0.9 to 1.35 kg); wingspan 23.0 to 37.0 inches (82.0 to 95.0 cm). Male has iridescent green head, rusty chest, and gray body. Female is mottled brown. Iridescent blue patch on wings of both sexes. Most widespread and abundant duck in North America.

**Track:** Four toes. Toes 2 to 4, which point forward, usually register. Toe 1 points rearward and may not show. Distal webbing between toes 2, 3, and 4. Webbing concave between toes. Toes 2 and 4 tend to converge near tips. Claws are broad, blunt, and attached to toes. Feet turned in.

**Trail:** Walking stride about 4.0 inches (10.0 cm).

**scat**
2.0 x 0.25 in
5.0 x 0.6 cm

SCAT WIDTH

**Scat:** Pencil-size cords, four to eight times longer than wide. Often greenish and coated with white nitrogenous deposits.

**Habitat:** Ponds, lakes, marshes, streams, rivers, and bays.

**Similar species:** Differs from geese and swans by smaller size. Differs from pelicans and cormorants by lacking webbing between toes 1 and 2. Differs from gulls by having convergent toes.

**Other sign:** Nests may be on the ground, in tree cavities, or on floating mats. Eggs roughly the size of chicken eggs, though there may be great variation among species.

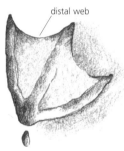

distal web

**feet**
2.2 x 2.4 in
5.5 x 6.0 cm

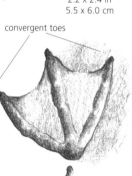

convergent toes

**walk**

TRACK LENGTH

TRACK WIDTH

# Lesser Scaup
*Aythya affinis*

Aquatic bird, average length
**16.0 inches (40.0
cm). Male with dark
head iridescing
purple and green.
Dark, gray-black
body with white
sides. Small bill with a
small black tip. Female is brown with white at base of beak.**

**Track:** Four toes. Toes 2 to 4 point forward. Toe 1 points rearward and may not show. Distal webbing between toes 2, 3, and 4. Webbing concave between toes. Toes 2 and 4 tend to converge near tips. Claws are broad, blunt, and attached. Feet turn inward.

**Trail:** Walking stride is about 12.0 inches (30.0 cm).

**Scat:** Pencil-size cords, four to eight times longer than wide. Often greenish and coated with white nitrogenous deposits.

**scat**
1.5 x 0.25 in
3.8 x 0.6 cm

SCAT WIDTH

**Habitat:** A duck of ocean bays, estuaries, and freshwater lakes during the winter, it breeds in small bodies of water such as ponds, small lakes, and marshes.

**Similar species:** Differs from geese and swans by smaller size. Differs from pelicans and cormorants by lacking webbing between toes 1 and 2. Differs from gulls by having convergent toes.

**Other sign:** Nest is lined with down and placed in a hollow in the grass.

distal web

**feet**
2.0 x 2.2 in
5.0 x 5.5 cm

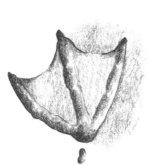

**walk**

*TRACK LENGTH*

*TRACK WIDTH*

# Canada Goose
*Branta canadensis*

Medium-size
aquatic bird, average
length 30.0 inches (75.0
cm). Considerable size
variation among sub-
species. Black head and
neck, with a white chin
band. Back is olive
brown. Male and female
similarly colored.

**Track:** Four toes. Toes 2 to 4, which point forward, usually register. Toe 1 points rearward and only occasionally shows. Distal webbing between toes 2, 3, and 4. Toes 2 and 4 tend to converge slightly near tips. Claws are broad, blunt, and usually attached to toes. Feet turn in.

**Trail:** Walking stride is about 12.0 inches (30.0 cm).

**scat**
3.0 x 0.4 in
7.5 x 1.0 cm

SCAT WIDTH

**Scat:** Cord, five to eight times longer than wide. As long as 3.5 inches (8.8 cm). Often greenish and coated with white nitrogenous deposits.

**Habitat:** Ponds, lakes, marshes, streams, rivers, and bays.

**Similar species:** Larger than most ducks and smaller than swans. Differs from pelican and cormorant by lacking webbing between toes 1 and 2. Larger than gulls, and differing from them by having convergent toes and distal webbing.

**Other sign:** Nests on ground, sometimes on cliff ledges, and in abandoned heron and raptor nests. Eggs larger than chicken eggs.

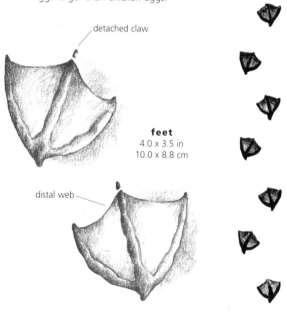

detached claw

distal web

**feet**
4.0 x 3.5 in
10.0 x 8.8 cm

**walk**

TRACK LENGTH

TRACK WIDTH

# Red-tailed Hawk
*Buteo jamaicensis*

Medium-size bird, 18.0 to 26.0 inches (45.0 to 65.0 cm), 1.5 to 3.0 pounds (0.7 to 1.5 kg); wingspan 45.0 to 52.0 inches (114.0 to 133.0 cm). Female slightly larger than male. Highly variable, dark hawk with red tail feathers. Light phase has a dark belly band.

**Track:** Four wide, robust toes. Toes 2 to 4 point forward. Claws are long, sharp, and not attached to the toe print.

**Trail:** Walking stride is about 12.0 inches (30.0 cm). Hops or runs after prey on the ground. Claws may drag in soft mud, creating a fringe along sides of footprint.

**Scat:** Semiliquid, primarily white with some brown intermixed. Unlike owls, scat is ejected with force, sometimes leaving a trail. Whitish piles and vertical streaks below nests.

**cough pellets**

**Habitat:** Woodland and open country with scattered trees.

**Similar species:** Smaller than eagles. Differs from owls by having three toes pointing forward. Differs from geese and swans by lacking webbing. Differs from herons and cranes by having symmetrical feet.

**Other sign:** Cough pellets may be 1.5 to 4.0 inches (3.8 to 10.0 cm) long.

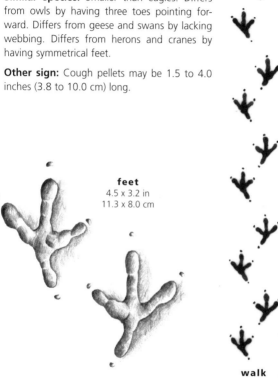

**feet**
4.5 x 3.2 in
11.3 x 8.0 cm

**walk**

# Bald and Golden Eagles
*Haliaeetus leucocephalus* and
*Aquila chrysaetos*

Large birds, averaging
35.0 inches (90.0 cm) in
length, with wingspans of
80.0 inches (200.0 cm).
Brown bodies. Adult
golden eagle (*Aquila
chrysaetos*) has golden feathers
over head and neck. Adult bald eagle
(*Haliaeetus leucocephalus*) has white
head, neck, and tail feathers.

**Bald eagle**
*Haliaeetus leucocephalus*

**Track:** Four wide, robust toes. Toes 2 to 4 point forward. Lacks webbing and metatarsal pad. Claws are long, sharp, and not attached to the toe print.

**Trail:** Walking stride about 18.0 inches (45.0 cm). Golden eagle will run after prey on the ground.

**Scat:** Semiliquid, primarily white with some brown intermixed.

**Habitat:** Golden eagle found in hilly areas and hunts over open country. Bald eagle usually found near lakes and rivers.

**cough pellet**

**urine stain on rock**

**Similar species:** Larger than hawk's track, which is less than 3.0 inches (7.5 cm). Differ from owls by having three toes pointing forward. Differ from geese and swans by lacking webbing. Differ from herons and cranes by having symmetrical feet.

**Other sign:** Cough pellets may be 5.0 x 1.5 inches (12.5 x 3.8 cm). Nests may be 6.0 feet (2.0 m) in diameter.

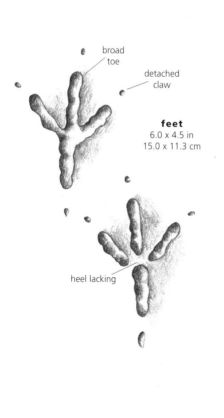

broad toe

detached claw

**feet**
6.0 x 4.5 in
15.0 x 11.3 cm

heel lacking

**walk**

# Blue Grouse
*Dendragapus obscurus*

**Chicken-size bird, averaging 18.0 inches (45.0 cm). Male is speckled gray, black, and white, with yellow eye combs and dark throat. Females are uniformly mottled brown.**

**Track:** Four toes, with toes 2 to 4 pointing out or forward. Toe 1, relatively short, may not show. Toes are relatively wide and lack webbing. Feet point forward to slightly inward. In a clear print, a narrow fringe of scales may show around toes. In winter, feathers on feet show.

**Trail:** Walking stride is about 9.5 inches (24.0 cm).

**Scat:** Light to dark brown, sometimes with white nitrogenous covering. Content includes buds, berries, and sawdust. In winter, scat accumulates in large mass of 50 or so in snow nest.

**Habitat:** Coniferous forest to the upper timberline.

**scat**
1.5 x 0.25 in
3.8 x 0.6 cm

*SCAT WIDTH*

**Similar species:** Differs from other forest birds by wide, robust toe size and short toe 1. Short stride and wide straddle of grouse trail different from other forest bird trails.

**Other sign:** Fly into or burrow under the snow to roost. Tunnel to nest makes a sharp turn, perhaps to confuse predators.

broad toe

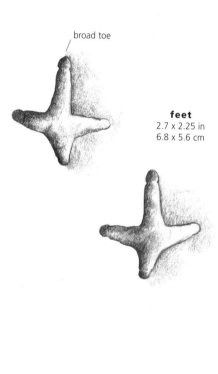

**feet**
2.7 x 2.25 in
6.8 x 5.6 cm

**walk**

TRACK LENGTH

TRACK WIDTH

# Spruce Grouse
*Dendragapus canadensis*

**Size comparable to a small chicken, 17.0 inches (43.0 cm) in length. A dark brown to gray-black bird with white spots on chest, especially the male. Orange tail feather tips, with red combs above eyes.**

**Track:** Four toes, with toes 2 to 4 pointing forward. Toe 1, relatively short, may not show. Toes are relatively wide and lack webbing. Claws detached. In winter, a fringe of scales makes toes wider.

**Trail:** Walking stride is about 9.0 inches (23.0 cm). Trail is straight and feet toe in. In deep snow, there can be a 4.0-inch (10.0-cm) wide trough. Look for wing marks in the snow as well as body impression under brush and evergreen trees.

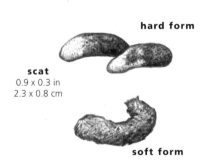

**hard form**

**scat**
0.9 x 0.3 in
2.3 x 0.8 cm

**soft form**

**Scat:** Light to dark brown, sometimes with white nitrogenous covering. Content includes buds, berries, and sawdust.

**Habitat:** Spruce forests with moss ground cover.

**Similar species:** Tracks larger than bobwhite. Differs from other forest birds by wide, robust toe size and short toe 1. Grouse trails can be differentiated from other forest birds by their short stride.

walk

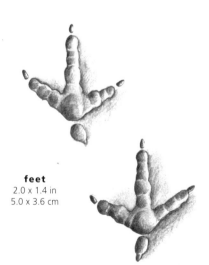

**feet**
2.0 x 1.4 in
5.0 x 3.6 cm

# Ruffed Grouse
*Bonasa umbellus*

**Chicken-size forest bird, 17.0 inches (43.0 cm) in length. Mottled brown in color. Black feather ruffs on side of neck. Wide, multibanded tail with dark band near tip.**

**Track:** Four toes, with toes 2 to 4 pointing forward. Toe 1, relatively short, may not show. Toes are relatively wide and lack webbing. Claws detached. In winter, a fringe of scales makes toes wider.

**Trail:** Walking stride is about 9.0 inches (23.0 cm). Trail is straight and feet toe in. In deep snow, there can be a trough, 4.0 inches (10.0 cm) wide. Look for wing marks in the snow as well as body impression under brush and evergreen trees.

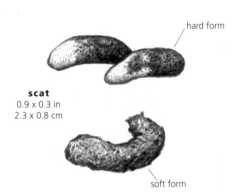

hard form

**scat**
0.9 x 0.3 in
2.3 x 0.8 cm

soft form

SCAT WIDTH

**Scat:** Light to dark brown, sometimes with white nitrogenous covering. Content includes buds, berries, and sawdust. In winter, deposited in snow nest in large mass of 50 or so scats. May be scattered if roosting in trees.

**Habitat:** Mixed deciduous woodlands with dense understory. Prefers aspen groves.

**Similar species:** Larger than bobwhite. Differs from other forest birds by wide, robust toe size and short toe 1. Grouse trails can be differentiated from other forest birds by their short stride.

**Other sign:** Burrow under the snow to roost. Round nests made from leaves and brush, usually 5.0 inches (13.0 cm) in diameter, made from leaves and brush. Dust baths in sandy areas.

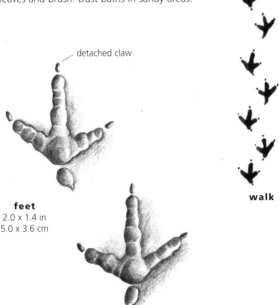

detached claw

**feet**
2.0 x 1.4 in
5.0 x 3.6 cm

**walk**

*TRACK LENGTH*

*TRACK WIDTH*

# Ring-necked Pheasant
*Phasianus colchicus*

Large, chickenlike bird, males 33.0 inches (84.0 cm) and females 21.0 inches (53.0 cm) in length. Male brightly colored with green head, mottled brown, black, bronze, and white body. Female is a mottled buffy brown. Male has a long, pointed tail.

**Track:** Four toes, with toes 2 to 4 pointing forward. Toe 1, relatively short, may not show. Toes are relatively wide and lack webbing. Feet point forward to slightly inward.

**Trail:** Walking stride is about 11.0 inches (28.0 cm). Narrow trail; toes neither toe in nor out.

**scat**
0.8 x 0.4 in
2.0 x 1.0 cm

SCAT WIDTH

**Scat:** Variable bulbous dropping, greenish brown with white ends. Sometimes two or more pieces sticking together.

**Habitat:** Bushy country, woodland edges, farmlands, and windrows.

**Similar species:** Differs from grouse by longer stride and narrower straddle. Smaller tracks differentiate from turkey.

**Other sign:** Nest in grass is a shallow depression occasionally lined with some grass.

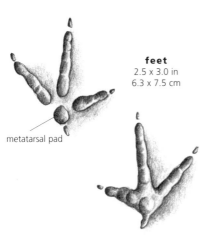

**feet**
2.5 x 3.0 in
6.3 x 7.5 cm

metatarsal pad

**walk**

TRACK LENGTH

TRACK WIDTH

# Ptarmigan
*Lagopus* species

At an average length of 14.0 inches (35.0 cm), larger than the American robin. Male and female similarly colored: brown- or black-and-white-mot-

**White-tailed Ptarmigan**
*Lagopus leucurus*

tled body in summer, with white on wings. All white in winter. Red eye combs. Three species, rock (*L. mutus*), willow (*L. Lagopus*), and white-tailed (*L. leucurus*), live in North America. They cannot be told apart by their tracks.

**Track:** Four toes, toes 2 to 4 pointing forward. Toe 1, relatively short, may not show. Toes are relatively wide and lack webbing. In winter the heavily feathered foot shows broad, diffuse toe imprints, and detail may be masked. Feet point forward to slightly inward.

**Trail:** Walking stride is about 6.0 inches (15.0 cm).

**scat**
1.25 x 0.25 in
3.1 x 0.6 cm

**snow nest and wing marks from takeoff**

SCAT WIDTH

**Scat:** Light to dark brown, sometimes with white nitrogenous covering. Includes buds, berries, and sawdust. About 1.5 inches (3.8 cm) long. In winter, deposited in snow nest in large mass of 50 or so scats.

**Habitat:** Rocky alpine slopes, meadows, and willow patches of high mountains.

**Similar species:** Differs from other forest birds by wide, robust toes and short toe 1. Trail shows short strides and wide straddle. Feathers on feet differentiate from other forest birds. Toe angle is narrower than grouse.

**Other sign:** Flies into or burrows under the snow to roost.

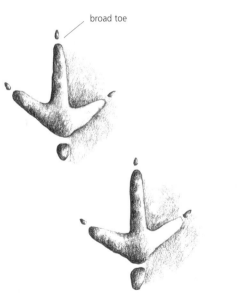

broad toe

**feet**
2.4 x 2.0 in
6.0 x 5.0 cm

**walk**

*TRACK LENGTH*

*TRACK WIDTH*

# Bobwhite
*Colinus virginianus*

**Size comparable to a small chicken, 9.0 inches (23.0 cm) in length. Mottled reddish brown with a short gray tail. Male with white stripes on face and throat, brownish in female.**

**Track:** Four toes, with toes 2 to 4 pointing forward. Toe 1, relatively short, may be detached or not show. Toes are relatively wide and lack webbing. Feet point forward to slightly inward.

**Trail:** Walking stride is about 6.0 inches (15.0 cm). Trail is straight, but feet toe in.

**Scat:** Light to dark brown, sometimes with white nitrogenous covering.

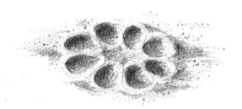

**depressions in dust from chicks**

**scat**
1.4 x 0.2 in
3.5 x 0.5 cm

*SCAT WIDTH*

**Habitat:** Tall grasslands, brushlands, open woodlands, and cultivated fields.

**Similar species:** Smaller than grouse. Differs from other forest birds by wide, robust toe size and short toe 1. Bobwhite trails can be differentiated from other forest birds by their short strides and wide straddles.

**Other sign:** Ground roost is a circle of shallow body depressions where birds sleep with their heads pointing out. Nest is a shallow depression under "woven" grass with a side entrance.

**walk**

**feet**
1.75 x 1.5 in
4.4 x 3.8 cm

*TRACK LENGTH*

*TRACK WIDTH*

# California Quail
*Callipepla californica*

**Small, chickenlike bird, average length 10.0 inches (25.0 cm). Gray-and-brown body, with short, black feather plume on head. White chest scales. Black-and-white pattern on face.**

**Track:** Four toes. Toes 2 to 4 point forward and slightly outward. Toes 3 and 4 nearly equal in length. Toe 1 detached, but usually registers. When it does, foot length is 2.0 inches (5.0 cm). Toes relatively wide; lack webbing. Claws attached.

**Trail:** Walking stride 8.0 to 10.0 inches (20.0 to 25.0 cm). Feet point slightly inward.

**Scat:** Long, thin cord, light to dark brown, occasionally with white nitrogenous covering. Quail's diet of dry vegetation causes scat texture to resemble sawdust. When dry, may break into small fragments.

**scat**
up to 0.6 x 0.1 in
up to 1.5 x 0.3 cm

**ground roost**

SCAT WIDTH

**Habitat:** Prefers edges of chaparral, woodlands, shrublands, parks, and farms.

**Similar species:** Differs from grouse by having less robust tracks, narrower toes, and toe 2 tending to be shorter than toes 3 and 4. Tracks are clearer than grouse, especially in winter, as quail lacks toe feathers. Toes broader than those of other ground-dwelling birds. Lack of webbing separates tracks from aquatic birds.

**Other sign:** Look for dust bath depressions along trails. Ground roosts form a circle of depressions where each bird's tail points into center.

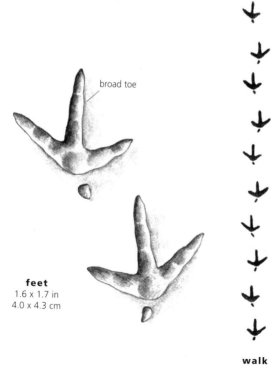

broad toe

**feet**
1.6 x 1.7 in
4.0 x 4.3 cm

walk

TRACK LENGTH

TRACK WIDTH

# Scaled Quail
*Callipepla squamata*

**Small, chickenlike bird, averaging 10.0 inches (25.0 cm). Gray back with brownish wings. White crest on head. Chest is scaled by black-edged feathers.**

**Track:** Four toes. Toes 2 to 4 point forward and slightly outward. Toes 3 and 4 nearly equal in length. Toe 1 detached, but usually registers. Toes relatively wide; lack webbing. Claws attached.

**Trail:** Walking stride 8.0 to 10.0 inches (20.0 to 25.0 cm). Feet point slightly inward.

**Scat:** Long, thin cord, light to dark brown, occasionally with white nitrogenous covering. Diet of dry vegetation causes scat texture to resemble sawdust. When dry, may break into small fragments.

**scat**
up to 0.6 x 0.1 in
up to 1.5 x 0.3 cm

**ground roost**

SCAT WIDTH

**Habitat:** Arid grasslands, plains, and open shrubland. Wide range includes several species of quail.

**Similar species:** Differs from grouse by having less robust tracks, narrower toes, and toe 2 tending to be shorter than toes 3 and 4. Tracks are clearer than grouse, especially in winter, as quail lacks toe feathers. Toes broader than those of other ground-dwelling birds. Lack of webbing separates tracks from aquatic birds.

**Other sign:** Look for dust bath depressions along trails. Ground roosts form a circle of depressions where each bird's tail points into center.

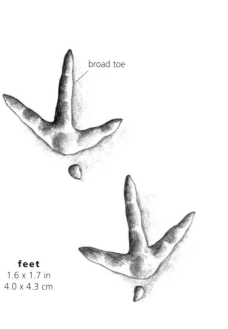

broad toe

**feet**
1.6 x 1.7 in
4.0 x 4.3 cm

**walk**

*TRACK LENGTH*

*TRACK WIDTH*

# Turkey
*Meleagris gallopavo*

Large, ground-dwelling bird. Males average 45.0 inches (113.0 cm) and females 35.0 inches (88.0 cm) in length. Smaller and more slender than the domesticated Thanksgiving turkey. Male has a dark-brown to black body, with white stripes on flight feather; tail feathers are tipped with brownish white. Color of female's feathers is similar but dull. Male also has red *wattles*, folds of skin hanging from the chin.

**Track:** Four broad, robust toes. Toes 2 to 4 face forward. Hind toe (toe 1) only occasionally registers, and then in a straight line with toe 4. Only the claw or tip of toe 1 registers. Metatarsal pad present, though it may be unattached to toes. Claws narrow and usually attached to toe.

**Trail:** Walking stride 15.0 inches (38.0 cm). Foot axis may vary, pointing into the line of travel or turning slightly out.

**scat**
3.0 x 0.5 in
7.5 x 1.3 cm

**tracks with scratch marks**

SCAT WIDTH

**Scat:** Solid scat is long, up to 3.0 inches (7.5 cm), narrow, and brown with greenish-white nitrogenous material on ends. Also produces a soft scat that piles in a shapeless mass on ground.

**Habitat:** Open forest, shrubland, and wooded swamps, in trees with lateral branches for roosting at night.

**Similar species:** Differs from other birds by wide, robust toes. Tracks larger than other ground-dwelling birds. Lacks webbing of ducks and certain other aquatic birds. Separated from eagles by presence (usually) of metatarsal pad. Toes 2 and 4 point forward to a greater degree than those of crane.

**Other sign:** Scratches on ground where turkey digs for seeds, acorns, nuts, and insects.

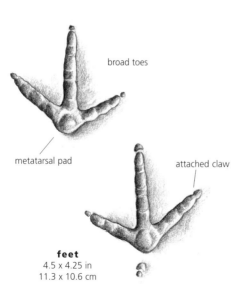

broad toes

metatarsal pad

attached claw

**feet**
4.5 x 4.25 in
11.3 x 10.6 cm

**walk**

TRACK LENGTH

TRACK WIDTH (50%)

# Coot
*Fulica americana*

**Medium-size aquatic bird, average length 15.0 inches (38.0 cm). Slate-black body, with white beak extending into small brown forehead shield.**

**Track:** Four toes showing, toes 2 to 4 pointing forward. Toe 1 angles inward. Toes 2, 3, and 4 have fringe of webbing with indented lobes. Long, pointed claws, especially those on toe 1, may be separated from toes.

**Trail:** Walking stride 10.0 inches (25.0 cm); tends to wander when walking. Foot axis parallel to line of travel.

**Scat:** White liquid.

**Habitat:** Freshwater lakes and ponds having shallow water where reeds and rushes grow.

**Similar species:** Differs from all other aquatic birds by the indented lobes on each toe.

**Other sign:** Floating nest built from cattails, sedges, and rushes, rising several inches above the water.

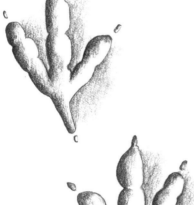

**feet**
5.2 x 4.8 in
13.0 x 12.0 cm

**walk**

TRACK LENGTH

TRACK WIDTH (50%)

# Sandhill Crane
*Grus canadensis*

**Large bird, average length 39.0 inches (98.0 cm). Appearance of males and females similar: grayish, with red crown on head and white cheeks and chin.**

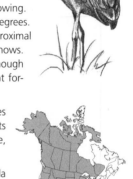

**Track:** Four toes, toes 2 to 4 showing. Outside toes opposed by nearly 180 degrees. Toe 3 is longer than 2 and 4. Small proximal web between toes 2 and 3 rarely shows. Claws usually attached to toes, though claw of toe 1 rarely shows. Feet point forward.

**Trail:** Walking stride about 24.0 inches (60.0 cm). Often runs, extending its stride. Tracks have a narrow straddle, being nearly in line with one another.

**Scat:** Similar to, but smaller than, Canada goose. Brown in color, with some vegetation. Can contain bones of small mammals, reptiles, and amphibians.

**Habitat:** Meadows, marshes, grasslands, and fields.

**scat**
2.5 x 0.3 in
6.3 x 0.8 cm

SCAT WIDTH

**Similar species:** Differs from ducks, geese, swans, and herons by having only small proximal web. Differs from large raptors by lacking toe 1.

**Other sign:** Listen for its rattling call, which suggests to some what dinosaurs may have sounded like.

**walk**

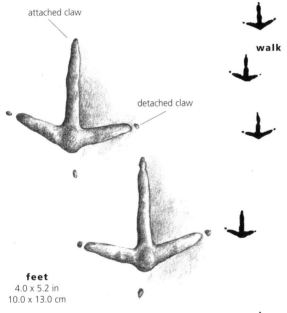

attached claw

detached claw

**feet**
4.0 x 5.2 in
10.0 x 13.0 cm

**run**

*TRACK LENGTH*

*TRACK WIDTH (50%)*

# Spotted Sandpiper
*Actitis macularia*

Medium-size shore-
bird with light yellow
legs and orange bill
with black tip or dark bill with
pale base. Back and head olive
brown, with white bar over eye;
underside white with distinct
round spots. Averages 7.0 to
8.0 inches (18.0 to 20.0 cm), 1.2 to
1.8 ounces (34.0 to 50.0 g); wingspan
15.0 to 16.0 inches (37.0 to 40.0 cm).
Female larger, with larger spots
extending farther down on belly.

**Track:** Four narrow toes, although toe 1
may not show. Toes 2 to 4 face forward
and are nearly symmetrical around toe 3.
Outer toe angle often greater than 120
degrees. Small, proximal webbing between toes 2, 3, and 4 may
be visible, though curlews and sandpipers have proximal webbing
only between toes 3 and 4.

**Trail:** Shorebirds are constantly running along the water's edge.

**beach with beak holes**

**Scat:** Small and semiliquid. Brown, green, and white mixed.

**Habitat:** Water's edge at lakes, rivers, streams, wastewater treatment plants.

**Similar species:** Differs from song- or perching birds by the weak showing of toe 1, which in perching birds is strong and used to grasp branches. Outer toe angle of songbirds is less than 90 degrees. Shorebirds walk, but most songbirds hop.

**Other sign:** Myriad roundish holes where beak pushed into the sand in pursuit of insects.

**feet**
1.25 x 1.0 in
3.1 x 2.5 cm

**walk**

# Avocet
*Recurvirostra americana*

Long-legged shore-
bird with strongly
upcurved black bill and blue-gray
legs. Female's bill more strongly
upcurved. Bold black-and-white
pattern on back and wings, with
gray head; white rump and tail.
Breeding plumage, rusty reddish
brown along head and back. Averages
18.0 inches (45.0 cm), 12.0 ounces (336.0 g);
wingspan 9.0 inches (22.5 cm).

**Track:** Four narrow toes, although toe 1 may not show. Toes 2 to 4 face forward and are nearly symmetrical around toe 3. Outer toe angle often greater than 120 degrees. Mesial webbing between toes 2, 3, and 4 may be visible.

**Trail:** Shorebirds are constantly running along the water's edge. Stride 7.0 inches (18.0 cm). Toe 3 parallel to line of travel.

**Scat:** Small and semiliquid. Brown, green, and white mixed.

**Habitat:** Water's edge at lakes, rivers, streams, bays, and waste-water treatment plants.

**nest in grass
with twigs**

**Similar species:** Differs from song- or perching birds by the weak showing of toe 1, which in perching birds is strong and used to grasp branches. Outer toe angle of songbirds is less than 90 degrees. Shorebirds walk or run, but most songbirds hop.

**Other sign:** Myriad roundish holes where beak pushed into the sand in pursuit of insects.

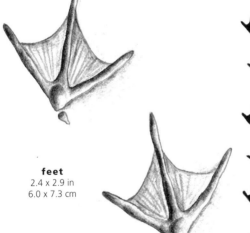

**feet**
2.4 x 2.9 in
6.0 x 7.3 cm

may not show

**walk**

*TRACK LENGTH*

*TRACK WIDTH*

# Herring Gull
*Larus argentatus*

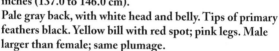

Gregarious species of open beaches of lakes, oceans, and rivers; found throughout North America. Average length 22.0 to 26.0 inches (56.0 to 66.0 cm), 1.75 to 2.75 pounds (0.8 to 1.3 kg); 54.0 to 57.0 inches (137.0 to 146.0 cm).
Pale gray back, with white head and belly. Tips of primary feathers black. Yellow bill with red spot; pink legs. Male larger than female; same plumage.

**Track:** Four toes. Toes 2 to 4 (forward-pointing) show. Toe 1 may register only slightly or not show at all. Webbing relatively straight between toes. Toes 2 and 3 tend to diverge, especially at the tips.

**Trail:** Walking stride about 13.0 inches (33.0 cm). Feet turn slightly inward.

**Scat:** Semiliquid. Primarily white, with indistinguishable contents.

**cough pellet**

**Habitat:** Along coast and on inland lakes and rivers. Nest in colonies on ground or cliffs, usually on islands. Nest is made of grass or seaweed. A scavenger. Also found at dumps.

**Similar species:** Differs from ducks, swans, and geese by having divergent toes. Smaller than swans and geese. Differs from coot by having webbing between toes. Great variation exists among gull species.

**Other sign:** Cough pellets containing bones, fish scales, urchin parts, and garbage. Shell fragments from dropping mussel shells onto rocks from high in the air.

toes 2 and 4 diverge

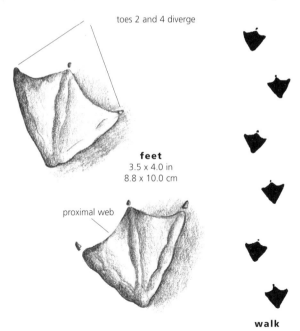

**feet**
3.5 x 4.0 in
8.8 x 10.0 cm

proximal web

**walk**

*TRACK LENGTH*

*TRACK WIDTH (50%)*

# California Gull
*Larus californicus*

Medium-size bird of the lake edges, average length 8.0 to 10.0 inches (20.0 to 25.0 cm). Adult male and female similarly colored: medium gray on back and wings, wing feathers tipped with black. Yellow legs, white chest and head. Yellow bill with red and black.

**Track:** Four toes. Only toes 2 to 4 (forward-pointing) show. Distal webbing between toes 2, 3, and 4. Webbing relatively straight between toes. Toes 2 and 3 tend to diverge, especially at tips. Feet turned slightly inward.

**Trail:** Walking stride is 4.0 inches (10.0 cm).

**Scat:** Semiliquid. Primarily white, with indistinguishable contents.

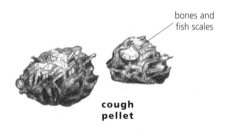

bones and fish scales

**cough pellet**

**Habitat:** Mountain lakes, cultivated fields, and landfills.

**Similar species:** Differs from ducks, swans, and geese by having divergent toes. Smaller than swans and geese. Differs from coot by having webbing between toes. Great variations in stride exist among gull species.

**Other sign:** Cough pellets are up to 4.0 inches (10.0 cm) long. Pellets include a variety of materials, reflecting the gull's omnivorous diet.

toes 2 and 4 diverge

**feet**
1.4 x 1.6 in
3.5 x 4.0 cm

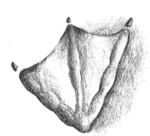

**walk**

*TRACK LENGTH*

*TRACK WIDTH*

# Roadrunner
*Geococcyx californianus*

Medium-size, ground-dwelling cuckoo, averaging 23.0 inches (60.0 cm) that runs rapidly and seldom flies. Brown-and-white-streaked body with a dark crest. Long tail, tipped with white.

**Track:** Four relatively long, slender toes. Toes 1 and 4 point backward. Toes 1 and 4 similar in length to toes 2 and 3. Claws on toes 2 and 3 detached and prominent. Claws on toes 1 and 4 usually do not register.

**Trail:** Running stride averages 16.0 inches (40.0 cm), but may be considerably longer as the roadrunner can leave the ground in midstride.

**Scat:** I have not observed their scat.

**Habitat:** Shrub desert including mesquite and chaparral.

**Similar species:** Four toes, with two pointing forward includes ospreys, owls, cuckoos, kingfishers, and four-toed woodpeckers. Woodpecker track distinct in that toes 1 and 4 are not similar in length to toes 2 and 3. Toes 2 and 3 of the kingfisher are closely joined by webbing. Osprey and owl tracks have broader, more robust toes. Habitat is a good clue to identification.

**Other sign:** Nest in low thicket or cactus may contain snake skins and mammal feces.

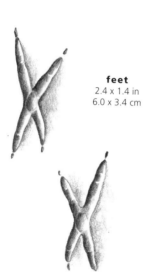

**feet**
2.4 x 1.4 in
6.0 x 3.4 cm

**walk**

*TRACK LENGTH*

*TRACK WIDTH*

# Owls
various species

Considerable variation in length, from the saw-whet owl (*Aegolius acadicus*), 8.0 inches (20.0 cm), to the short-eared owl (*Asio flammeus*) illustrated here, 15.0 inches (38.0 cm), to the great horned owl (*Bubo virginianus*), 25.0 inches (63.0 cm). All species have immobile eyes offset by facial disks of feathers. Great variability in appearance between species. Typical body colors are grays, browns, and reddish browns.

**Short-eared owl**
*Asio flammeus*

**Track:** Four broad toes, with two paired and facing forward. Toe 4 position is not fixed and may face back or out. Lack webbing and metatarsal pads. Claws long and detached from footprint. Tracks of short-eared owl illustrated here.

**Trail:** Walking stride varies considerably among species, from 3.0 to 10.0 inches (7.5 to 25.0 cm).

**cough pellet**

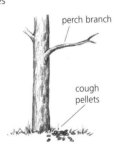

perch branch

cough pellets

**perch with pellets**

**Scat:** Semiliquid, primarily white.

**Habitat:** Forested areas. Some species, such as barn owls, will readily use human structures.

**Similar species:** Differ from most birds in toes 2 and 3 being paired, nearly parallel, and pointing forward. Differ from woodpeckers by toes being wide and robust, and by toes 1 and 4 being much shorter than toes 2 and 3.

**Other sign:** Cough pellets below a roost. Diameter of cough pellets ranges from 0.25 to 1.0 inch (0.6 to 2.5 cm) and is directly related to the size of the owl. Pellets are shiny and black when new but turn gray with age.

detached claw

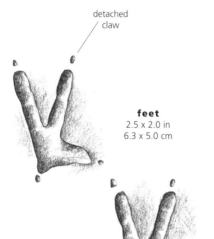

**feet**
2.5 x 2.0 in
6.3 x 5.0 cm

**walk**

TRACK LENGTH

TRACK WIDTH

# Northern Flicker
*Colaptes auratus*

**Medium-size woodpecker, slightly larger than the American robin, average length 12.0 inches (30.0 cm). Male has brown-barred back, black chest, white rump, and red or black whisker stripe, and is yellow under wings. Female lacks whisker stripe.**

**Track:** Four toes, with two parallel and pointing forward. Toes 1 and 4 point backward and are not equal in length. Strong, rigid tail feathers may show on ground.

**Trail:** Walking stride is about 3.0 inches (7.5 cm). Hopping stride is about 4.0 inches (10.0 cm).

**Scat:** Cord, about four or more times longer than wide. Often contains undigested parts of insects.

**Habitat:** Open woodlands, dense forests, and around towns.

**Similar species:** Differs from three-toed woodpecker by presence of toe 1. Differs from other birds its size by having two toes pointing forward.

**scat**
1.0 x 0.25 in
2.5 x 0.6 cm

SCAT WIDTH

**Other sign:** Excavates and nests in tree cavities. Does not add bedding material to cavity nest.

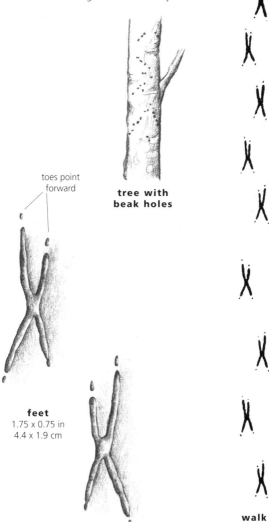

tree with
beak holes

toes point
forward

**feet**
1.75 x 0.75 in
4.4 x 1.9 cm

**walk**

TRACK LENGTH

TRACK WIDTH

# Crow
*Corvus brachyrhynchos*

**Medium-size (17.0 inches/43.0 cm) black bird with strong beak (smaller than raven's). Sides of tail are parallel in flight, not wedge shaped. Black feet and legs.**

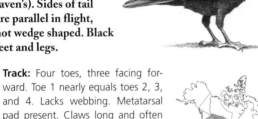

**Track:** Four toes, three facing forward. Toe 1 nearly equals toes 2, 3, and 4. Lacks webbing. Metatarsal pad present. Claws long and often detached from footprint. The footprint length of 2.5 inches (6.3 cm) includes toe 4, which adds 0.7 inch (1.8 cm).

**Trail:** Walking stride varies but is about 5.0 inches (13.0 cm). Crows both walk and hop and may run with a long stride.

**Scat:** Semiliquid brown and white, but may contain remnants of food from their omnivorous diet.

**cough pellet**

**Habitat:** Roadside, woodlands, farms, orchards, and lake and ocean shores.

**Similar species:** Raven track and trail is much larger than crow's. Lacks the paired forward-facing toes of owls. Lacks long toe 1 of hawks.

**Other sign:** Cough pellets up to 1.0 x 0.4 inch (2.5 x 1.0 cm). Pellets may contain berries, seeds, nuts, insect parts, and snails, among other items of its varied diet.

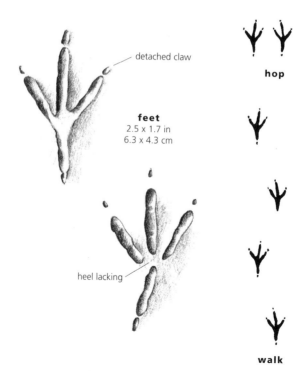

detached claw

**feet**
2.5 x 1.7 in
6.3 x 4.3 cm

heel lacking

hop

walk

TRACK LENGTH

TRACK WIDTH

# Blue Jay
*Cyanocitta cristata*

**Small bird with blue
body and white
markings on wings.
Prominent blue
crest and black throat band.
Average length
11.0 inches (28.0 cm).**

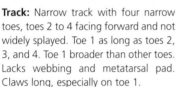

**Track:** Narrow track with four narrow toes, toes 2 to 4 facing forward and not widely splayed. Toe 1 as long as toes 2, 3, and 4. Toe 1 broader than other toes. Lacks webbing and metatarsal pad. Claws long, especially on toe 1.

**Trail:** Hopping stride is 4.0 to 5.0 inches (10.0 to 12.5 cm). Occasionally walks.

**Scat:** Semiliquid, brown to black with white intermixed.

**Habitat:** Woodlands, gardens, and parks.

**Similar species:** Differs from songbirds by larger size and relatively narrow footprint. Smaller and narrower than crows and ravens.

**Other sign:** Nest, on horizontal branch or tree crotch, is compact and occasionally cemented with mud.

**hop**

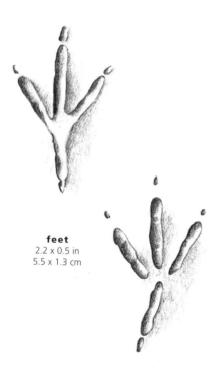

**feet**
2.2 x 0.5 in
5.5 x 1.3 cm

**walk**

TRACK LENGTH

TRACK WIDTH

# Gray Jay
*Perisoreus canadensis*

Small bird with gray body, blackish nape, and black beak. Average length 11.0 inches (28.0 cm). This friendly bird, whose food-foraging habits earned it the name camp robber, will eat from your hand. Anthropologists tell us that butchered bones indicate gray jays have been at our campfires for nearly 9,000 years.

**Track:** Narrow track with four narrow toes, toes 2 to 4 facing forward and not widely splayed. Toe 1 as long as toes 2, 3, and 4. Toe 1 broader than other toes. Lacks webbing and metatarsal pad. Claws long, especially on toe 1.

**Trail:** Hopping stride is 4.0 to 5.0 inches (10.0 to 12.5 cm). Occasionally walks.

**Scat:** Semiliquid, brown to black with white intermixed.

**Habitat:** Coniferous trees where it feeds on seeds, insects, and even carrion.

**Similar species:** Differs from songbirds by larger size and relatively narrow footprint. Smaller and narrower than crows and ravens.

**Other sign:** Nest, on horizontal branch or tree crotch, is compact and occasionally cemented with mud.

**hop**

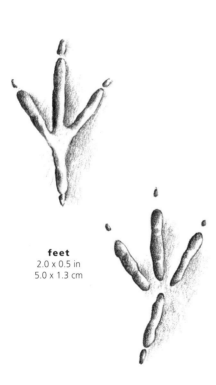

**feet**
2.0 x 0.5 in
5.0 x 1.3 cm

**walk**

*TRACK LENGTH*

*TRACK WIDTH*

# Black-billed Magpie
*Pica pica*

Black and iridescent
green body, wings,
and unusually long
tail. Average length
20.0 inches (50.0 cm).
Belly is white. Beak is
black.

**Track:** Four medium-wide toes,
three facing forward. Toe 1 nearly
as long as toes 2, 3, and 4. Lacks
webbing and metatarsal pad. Claws
long and detached from footprint.

**Trail:** Walking stride is about 6.0
inches (15.0 cm).

**Scat:** Semiliquid, brown with white
intermixed.

**cough pellet**

**Habitat:** Lower mountains, in open woodlands, thickets, along stream edges. Often found near human habitation.

**Similar species:** Differs from songbirds by larger size and relatively wide toes. Smaller than crows and ravens.

**Other sign:** Caches food in trees and under bark. Cough pellets are 1.25 x 0.4 inches (3.2 x 1.0 cm).

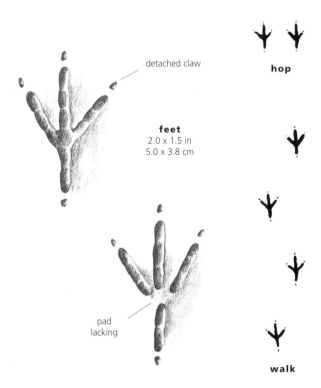

detached claw

**hop**

**feet**
2.0 x 1.5 in
5.0 x 3.8 cm

pad
lacking

**walk**

*TRACK LENGTH*

*TRACK WIDTH*

# Common Raven
*Corvus corax*

Large black bird, length averaging 24.0 inches (60.0 cm). Beak heavy. Tail is wedge shaped in flight. Size varies considerably, though male is larger than female.

**Track:** Four toes, toes 2 to 4 facing forward. Length of toe 1 nearly equals toes 2, 3, and 4. Lacks webbing and metatarsal pad. Claws long and detached from footprint.

**Trail:** Walking stride varies considerably, but is about 20.0 inches (50.0 cm). Also runs, with a longer stride.

**Scat:** Semiliquid; brown, black, and white. Often oily. May contain remnants of its omnivorous diet.

**Habitat:** Mountains, especially where carcasses of deer and elk can be found, and at garbage dumps. Will beg food from picnickers.

**cough pellet**

**Similar species:** Track and trail of the common crow are diminutive versions of the raven's. Lacks the paired forward-facing toes of owls. Lacks the long toe 1 of hawk's. Smaller than eagle's.

**Other sign:** Cough pellets up to 3.0 x 0.5 inches (7.5 x 1.3 cm). Caches food in forks of trees and, often, by burying.

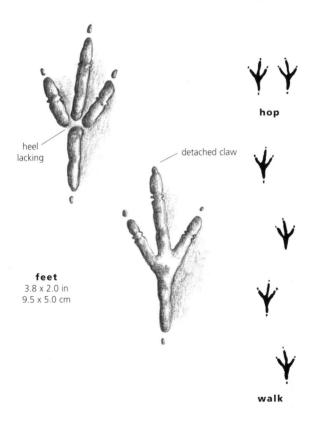

heel
lacking

detached claw

**feet**
3.8 x 2.0 in
9.5 x 5.0 cm

**hop**

**walk**

# American Robin
*Turdus migratorius*

Perhaps the most recognized North American bird, the robin is a small bird with a dark gray back and orange chest and stomach. The head is darker, with a white ring around the eye. Average length is 10.0 inches (25.0 cm).

**Track:** Four toes, toes 2 to 4 facing forward. Length of toe 1 nearly equals toes 2 and 4. Toe 3 is longer than 1 and bulbous at end. Outer toes spread. Lacks webbing and metatarsal pad. Claws short and may be detached from footprint.

**Trail:** Walking stride varies considerably, but is about 3.0 inches (7.5 cm). Also runs, with a longer stride.

**Scat:** Semiliquid to pasty and white.

**Habitat:** Open woodland habitat to urban areas. Uses conifer or deciduous trees for nesting. Usually seen in the grass searching for earthworms.

**Similar species:** Differs from songbirds by wide spreading toes, creating a relatively wide, curving footprint. Smaller and narrower than jays and crows, whose toes do not splay.

**Other sign:** Cough pellets up to 3.0 x 0.5 inches (7.5 x 1.3 cm). Caches food in forks of trees and, often, by burying.

**hop**

**feet**
2.0 x 1.0 in
5.0 x 2.5 cm

**walk**

*TRACK LENGTH*

*TRACK WIDTH*

# Opossum
*Didelphis marsupialis*

The size of a large
domestic cat, but
more stout; nearly
hairless, and with
a round, ratlike tail.
Weight varies from 8.0 to
14.0 pounds (3.5 to 6.5 kg).
Face whitish, with thin black-
edged ears. Body is whitish with gray
and black hairs interspersed.

**Track:** Five toes. Hind print is distinctive, with an opposable (like the human thumb) inside toe protruding sideways from other toes. Outside toe is slightly separated from middle three toes. Front footprint is wider than long and shows long toes that widen slightly toward the end.

**Trail:** Walking stride 18.0 inches (45.0 cm). Walking trail often reflects slow movement, with hind footprint registering behind the front. Trail is sloppy, and footprints seldom register directly. Tail drag often shows. Walking pattern occasionally similar to that of the raccoon, where the hind footprint registers beside the front footprint.

scat shape is highly variable

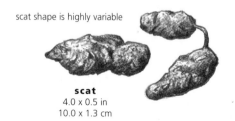

**scat**
4.0 x 0.5 in
10.0 x 1.3 cm

SCAT WIDTH

**Scat:** Highly variable shape and size and lack of distinctive form reflect highly variable, omnivorous diet. Single scat may be up to 4.0 inches (10.0 cm) long.

**Habitat:** Prefers riparian areas, woodlands, and farmyards. Habitat is not restricted by diet, as the opossum will eat small mammals, birds, eggs, reptiles, amphibians, fish, carrion, fruit, and any garbage it can find.

**Similar species:** Trail may be confused with muskrats, woodrats, and domestic rats when a tail drag is present. However, the distinctive hind footprint and large size of the opossum footprint identify its trail.

**Other sign:** Dens in logs, stumps, rock crevices, and dens of other animals.

**amble**

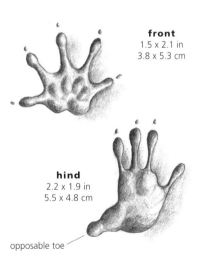

**front**
1.5 x 2.1 in
3.8 x 5.3 cm

**hind**
2.2 x 1.9 in
5.5 x 4.8 cm

opposable toe

**walk**

FRONT TRACK LENGTH

FRONT TRACK WIDTH

# Shrews
various species

**Masked shrew**
*Sorex cinereus*

Smaller than mice, less
than 0.25 ounce (7.0/g).
Long, pointed nose.
Minute eyes and ears.
Color brown to black,
with gray to white belly. Eat
mostly insects. The masked shrew
(*Sorex cinereus*) is illustrated here.

**Track:** Five slender toes are present on front and hind feet. In clear prints, four interdigital and two proximal pads may be seen.

**Trail:** Hopping stride seldom more than 2.0 inches (5.0 cm). The group of tracks is less than 1.0 inch (2.5 cm) long. Seldom is the stride more than three times the group.

**Scat:** Usually small pellets with tapered ends.

**Habitat:** Found everywhere from grasslands to alpine areas. Look for tracks in wet, fine mud of riparian areas or in snow along logs

tapered ends

**scat**
0.08 in
0.2 cm

SCAT WIDTH

**insect remains**

or the edges of buildings. Wood piles and leaf litter make good homes.

**Similar species:** Differ from mice and voles by having five toes on front foot.

**Other sign:** After eating, leave body parts from insects they have killed. Often burrow just below the surface of the snow, opening tunnels that partially collapse and expose their route. Trails in the snow radiate from holes like spokes of a wheel.

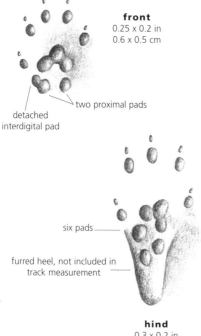

**front**
0.25 x 0.2 in
0.6 x 0.5 cm

two proximal pads

detached
interdigital pad

six pads

furred heel, not included in
track measurement

**hind**
0.3 x 0.2 in
0.8 x 0.5 cm

**bound**

*FRONT TRACK LENGTH*

*FRONT TRACK WIDTH*

# Armadillo
*Dasypus novemcinctus*

Size of a domestic cat, weighing 8.0 to 17.0 pounds (3.5 to 8.0 kg). Body, tail, and head are covered with a horny armor derived from the leathery skin. A few hairs are found between scales. Body color a light tan to gray. Large gray to black ears.

**Track:** Front tracks with four toes, hind with five. Often only the prominent inner toes, two on front, three on rear, register. Claws are prominent and broad, may appear attached, and usually dig deeply into the ground.

**Trail:** Trotting stride is about 25.0 inches (65.0 cm), walking stride around 15.0 inches (40.0 cm). Uses side gaits including trots and lopes. Occasionally the belly or tail drags.

**Scat:** Usually elongate, but may be spherical. Usually contains insect remains and a considerable amount of dirt.

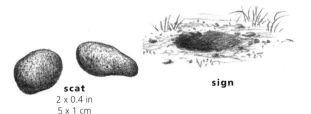

**scat**
2 x 0.4 in
5 x 1 cm

**sign**

**Habitat:** Usually dry, sandy areas, including brush, woodlands, and chaparral. Seems to additionally prefer rocky areas and cliffs.

**Similar species:** Easily separated from other mammals by prominent claws and odd numbers of toes in tracks.

**Other sign:** Digs out ant mounds and disturbs ground litter as it roots for insects. Digs long dwelling burrows that are around 8.0 inches (20.0 cm) in diameter. Pulls vegetation into the burrows to form a nest.

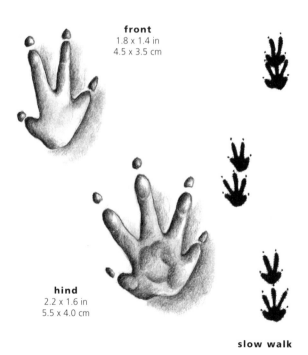

**front**
1.8 x 1.4 in
4.5 x 3.5 cm

**hind**
2.2 x 1.6 in
5.5 x 4.0 cm

**slow walk**

*FRONT TRACK LENGTH*

*FRONT TRACK WIDTH*

# Red Fox
*Vulpes vulpes*

Border collie–
size, 6.0
to 15.0
pounds
(3.0 to 7.0 kg).
Reddish yellow, with
black stockings and
a white tip on the
tail. Regional color phases include silver, black, cross, and
bluish gray. Long, pointed ears and elongate, pointed muzzle.

**Track:** Claws prominent. One lobe on the leading edge of the interdigital pad. Inside toe slightly larger than outside. A ridge of callus present across interdigital pad, but difficult to detect on hind footprint. Front foot larger than hind.

**Trail:** Trotting stride averages 32.0 inches (80.0 cm). Typically uses a trotting gait and, occasionally, a 2 x 2 trot with body turned to the side. Walks more than coyote, especially in shrubs.

**Scat:** Often has tapered tail. Composition varies. Mouse or rabbit fur, berries, and insects are common. Bird feathers and plant remains often present.

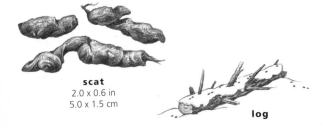

**scat**
2.0 x 0.6 in
5.0 x 1.5 cm

**log**

SCAT WIDTH

**Habitat:** Found in a variety of habitats from brush to croplands to mixed hard- and softwood forest. Prefers edges, where hunting for small mammals is good. Also found in urban areas, where cover is available during the daytime. Not found in dense forests.

**Similar species:** Differs from other canids by having a ridge of callus on the interdigital pad. Track tends to be larger than that of gray fox, and usually shows claws. Differs from bobcat in having only one lobe on the interdigital pad and claws (usually) showing.

**Other sign:** Multiple dens are used each season. Often digs own den. A given den may be used for several years. Look for small bones around den entrance. Scat has a diagnostic musky odor, produced by a musk gland on the top of the tail. Learn to identify this unique foxy odor. Foxes tightrope-walk on narrow logs. May take over woodchuck dens.

**side trot**

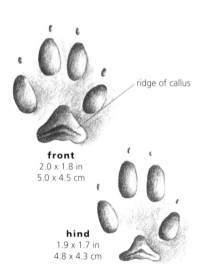

ridge of callus

**front**
2.0 x 1.8 in
5.0 x 4.5 cm

**hind**
1.9 x 1.7 in
4.8 x 4.3 cm

**trot**

FRONT TRACK LENGTH

FRONT TRACK WIDTH

# Gray Fox
*Urocyon cinereoargenteus*

Smaller than a border collie, 8.0 to 11.0 pounds (4.0 to 5.0 kg). Body color is pepper-and-salt. A black stripe runs down the back and upper side of tail. Sides are reddish. Tip of tail is black. Long, pointed ears and elongate, pointed muzzle.

**Track:** Small for a canid, somewhat broad and therefore somewhat cat-like. Claws, rarely present in track, are very small and sharp, giving the gray fox the ability to climb trees like a cat. Front foot larger than hind.

**Trail:** Generally a trot. Trotting stride averages 24.0 inches (60.0 cm). Walks more than coyote.

**Scat:** Often has tapered tail. Composition varies, as the gray fox is opportunistic when feeding. Rabbit fur is most common, followed by fur of other small mammals, berries, and insects. Plant remains are often present.

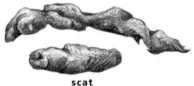

**scat**
2.0 x 0.6 in
5.0 x 1.5 cm

SCAT WIDTH

**Habitat:** Prefers a mixture of fields and woods. More often found in woodlands than is red fox. Early stage woodlands are preferred, with considerable activity in riparian habitats.

**Similar species:** Smaller than coyote and wolf. Lacks the ridge of callus on the interdigital pad of the red fox. Differs from coyote and red fox in that claws often do not show.

**Other sign:** Seldom digs dens, but makes use of woodpiles, rock outcrops, hollow trees, and brushpiles. Look for small bones around den entrances.

**side trot**

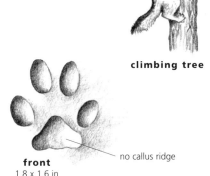

**climbing tree**

**front**
1.8 x 1.6 in
4.5 x 4.0 cm

— no callus ridge

**hind**
1.7 x 1.6 in
4.3 x 4.0 cm

**trot**

FRONT TRACK LENGTH

FRONT TRACK WIDTH

# Arctic Fox
*Alopex lagopus*

The size of a large domestic cat, 3.3 to 7.5 pounds (1.5 to 3.5 kg), with disproportionately small ears and legs. Two color forms, which change from summer to winter, exist: grayish brown (summer) to white (winter) and dark bluish gray or chocolate brown (summer) to bluish gray (winter). Large fluffy tail that acts like a weather vane in heavy wind, causing the fox to be blown parallel to the wind. Bottoms of feet are mostly hair-covered in winter.

**Track:** Small for a canid. Claws often do not show. Front foot larger than hind.

**Trail:** Generally lopes with a stride of 25.0 inches (64.0 cm). Hair-covered foot registers indistinctly in winter snow.

**Scat:** Usually has a tapered tail. Scat consists mostly of small mammals and birds, berries, and carrion.

**scat**
2.0 x 0.6 in
5.0 x 1.5 cm

SCAT WIDTH

**Habitat:** Hunts and scavenges along shore edges eating seabirds, eggs, and small mammals. Follows polar bears to scavenge off their kills.

**Similar species:** Smaller than coyote and red fox, whose claws show better. Lacks the ridge of callus on the interdigital pad of the red fox.

**Other sign:** Dens in burrows in the ground and snow. Forms or day beds on high and prominent ridges and rocks.

**lope**

**front**
about 2.0 x 1.9 in
5.0 x 4.8 cm

**hind**
1.8 x 1.7 in
4.6 x 4.3 cm

**walk**

*FRONT TRACK LENGTH*

*FRONT TRACK WIDTH*

# Kit and Swift Foxes
*Vulpes macrotis* and *V. velox*

Size of a domestic cat, 3.0 to 5.0 pounds (1.4 to 2.3 kg), with disproportionately large ears. Body color is pale red washed with gray. Tail has a black tip. The kit fox (*V. macrotis*), illustrated here, is found in the western portion of the range; the swift fox (*V. velox*), in the eastern part of the range. Some authors believe these foxes form a single species complex.

**Kit Fox**
*Vulpes macrotis*

**Track:** Small for a canid. Claws often do not show. Front foot larger than hind.

**Trail:** Walking stride 14.0 inches (35.0 cm). Loping stride 22.0 inches (55.0 cm). Dainty trail often mistaken for that of a cat. Details of footprint seldom register in sand.

**Scat:** Usually has a tapered tail. Scat consists mostly of small mammals and insects, but occasionally birds and reptiles.

**scat**
2.0 x 0.6 in
5.0 x 1.5 cm

**Habitat:** Found in sand habitats of the desert or plains where vegetation is sparse and short.

**Similar species:** Smaller than coyote, whose claws show better. Lacks the ridge of callus on the interdigital pad of the red fox. Tracks may be smaller than gray fox, although distinction may be difficult; the sand habitat is a good clue.

**Other sign:** Dens in burrows in the ground, where it hides during the day.

**front**
1.7 x 1.5 in
4.3 x 3.8 cm

**lope**

— no callus ridge

**hind**
1.3 x 1.2 in
3.3 x 3.0 cm

**walk**

FRONT TRACK LENGTH

FRONT TRACK WIDTH

# Coyote
*Canis latrans*

Collie-size canid,
20.0 to 25.0 pounds
(9.0 to 11.0 kg). Male
larger than female.
Color varies from completely
gray to tan to rust. Long,
pointed ears and long, narrow muzzle.

**Track:** Claws usually present. One lobe on the leading edge of the interdigital pad. Inside toe slightly larger than outside. Front foot larger than hind.

**Trail:** Trotting stride averages 41.0 inches (103.0 cm). Often uses a trot with body turned to the side, leaving a 2 x 2 track pattern. Often lopes, leaving a C-shaped pattern.

**Scat:** Varies from pure black animal protein to mostly hair with some bones. Tips tapered into long tails.

**Habitat:** An animal of the open brush country, the coyote digs its den on exposed hilltops or ridges with a view of surrounding area. Where persecuted, may den in a more secluded location.

**Similar species:** Even adult track is smaller than that of a two-month-old wolf pup. Track may overlap in size with red fox, but

**scat**
3.0 x 0.6 in
7.5 x 1.5 cm

SCAT WIDTH

lacks callus ridge of red fox. Track larger than gray fox, and usually shows claws. Differs from bobcat by showing claws and by having one lobe on leading edge of interdigital pad.

**Other sign:** Marks territory with urine and scat piles. Scat pile locations may be used repeatedly. Uses feet to scratch near scat piles, spreading odor from scat and foot glands to identify territory.

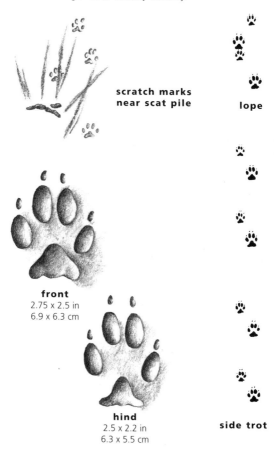

**scratch marks near scat pile**

**lope**

**front**
2.75 x 2.5 in
6.9 x 6.3 cm

**hind**
2.5 x 2.2 in
6.3 x 5.5 cm

**side trot**

*FRONT TRACK LENGTH*

*FRONT TRACK WIDTH*

# Wolf
*Canis lupus*

About German shepherd size, probably less than 100.0 pounds (45.0 kg). Male larger than female. Color varies from completely black to gray. Short, rounded ears and short, wide, blocky muzzle. The wolf apparently recolonizing the Northeast from Canada is a smaller member of the genus.

**Track:** Track about size of a softball. Claws usually present; one lobe on leading edge of interdigital pad. Inside toe slightly larger than outside. Front foot larger than hind.

**Trail:** Trotting stride averages 62.0 inches (155.0 cm). Often uses a C-shaped gallop or a trot with the body turned to the side, leaving a 2 x 2 pattern.

**Scat:** Varies from pure black, toothpastelike animal protein to mostly hair with some bones. Tips tapered into long tails.

**Habitat:** Found in all habitats. Tends to use cover when possible, moving in forest or at forest-meadow edge.

**scat**
4.0 x 1.25 in
10.0 x 3.2 cm

SCAT WIDTH

**Similar species:** Track larger than other canids. At 60 days of age, track larger than adult coyote's. Differs from mountain lion by having one lobe on the leading edge of the interdigital pad and usually showing claws. Differs from wolverine and bear by having only four toes, with the large toe on the inside.

**Other sign:** The alpha wolf, the dominant member of the pack, marks its territory by urinating on raised objects along the trail. Blood observed in the female's urine stain during January or February may indicate readiness to breed. Scratch marks beside urine stains or scat are territorial markings and are usually made with hind feet.

**side trot**

**urine mark of alpha wolf**

**front**
4.25 x 4.0 in
10.6 x 10.0 cm

**hind**
3.75 x 3.25 in
9.4 x 8.1 cm

**gallop**

*FRONT TRACK LENGTH*

*FRONT TRACK WIDTH (50%)*

# Jaguarundi
*Felis yagouaroundi*

Slightly larger than a domestic cat, 10.0 to 20.0 pounds (4.5 to 9.0 kg). Elongate shape, long tail, and short legs earned the name weasel cat. Ears are short, round, and widely set. Head is broad and flat. Two unspotted homogeneous color phases may exist in one litter—blackish to brownish gray or reddish yellow. Very rare in the United States.

**Track:** Front tracks are round or wider than long. Hind tracks longer than wide. Claw impressions are usually absent. Toes form a distinct arc, and toe 3 leads. The leading edge of the interdigital pad has two lobes. Inside toe distinctly larger than outside toe. Like the track of a large house cat. Measurements from two animals (one each Mexico and Texas) and literature.

**Trail:** Walking stride is about 13.0 inches (33.0 cm). Little else known.

**Scat:** No records, but probably typical of cat family. Uniform diameter cord with slight constrictions; ends usually blunt. When

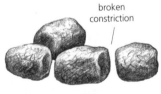

broken constriction

**scat**
3.6 x 0.4 in
9.0 x 1.0 cm

feeding on a dry diet, scat constricts and falls apart in short segments.

**Habitat:** Dense cover including thorny acacia and mesquite chaparral, and dry deciduous forests including scrub oak and sable palm.

**Similar species:** Cannot be definitively separated from a domestic cat. Smaller than other North American cats. Differs from those of fox by presence of two lobes on the anterior edge of the interdigital pad.

**Other sign:** None reported.

**walk**

**vertical leap
from
hind feet**

leading
toe

two lobes

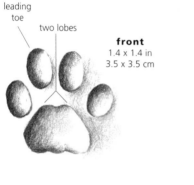

**front**
1.4 x 1.4 in
3.5 x 3.5 cm

**bound**

**hind**
1.1 x 1.0 in
2.7 x 2.6 cm

**walk**

*FRONT TRACK LENGTH*

*FRONT TRACK WIDTH*

# Ocelot
*Felis pardalis*

Collie-size,
weighing up to
35.0 lb (16.0 kg).
More slender than a
bobcat. Body color is
gray, buff, or cinna-
mon, with black-
rimmed, brown mark-
ings ranging in shape from
spots on body to stripes on neck.
Underside white with black markings.
Long tail marked with black stripes or
rings.

**Track:** Appears long for cats, with hind
tracks much longer than wide. Claw
impressions are usually absent. Toes form
a distinct arc, and toe 3 leads. The leading edge of the interdigital
pad has two lobes. Inside toe distinctly larger than outside toe.
Measurements from five ocelots from Texas.

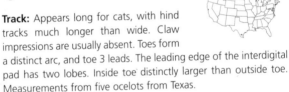

**sign**

broken
constriction

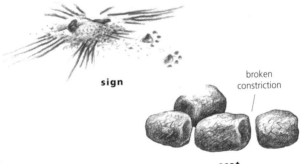

**scat**
3.0 x 0.8 in
7.5 x 2.0 cm

SCAT WIDTH

**Trail:** Trotting stride is about 40.0 inches (100.0 cm).

**Scat:** Tends to be constricted and, if dry, separates at constrictions into segments. Dry scat falls apart. Ends usually blunt. Scat from a fresh kill may form a uniform-diameter cord. Defecates at latrines, where feces accumulate.

**Habitat:** Seldom far from trees or dense cover. In Texas, found in dense, thorny chaparral of mesquite and acacia.

**Similar species:** Smaller than jaguar and lion, and larger than jaguarundi. Definitive characteristics are not available to separate ocelot tracks from bobcat. Differs from fox by presence of two lobes on the anterior edge of the interdigital pad.

**Other sign:** Probably scent marks with urine and scat. Scrapes dirt over scat. Scratches trees and fence posts.

**walk**

**vertical leap from hind feet**

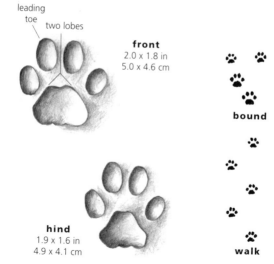

front
2.0 x 1.8 in
5.0 x 4.6 cm

leading toe — two lobes

hind
1.9 x 1.6 in
4.9 x 4.1 cm

**bound**

**walk**

*FRONT TRACK LENGTH*

*FRONT TRACK WIDTH*

# Bobcat
*Felis rufus*

Size of a collie, weighing 13.0 to 35.0 pounds (6.0 to 16.0 kg). Male larger than female. Overall color reddish to yellowish brown, with dark spots or streaks and whitish underside. Ears have tufts at tips. Back of ears and top of tail tip black. Tail is short or bobbed, about 4.0 inches (10.0 cm) long.

**Track:** Front track is round or wider than long. Hind track may be longer than wide. Claw impressions are usually absent. Toes form a slight arc and toe 3 leads. The leading edge of the interdigital pad has two lobes. Inside toe distinctly larger than outside toe.

**Trail:** Walking stride is about 20.0 inches (50.0 cm). Usually walks, but bounds with hind feet placed side by side when chasing prey. Winter trails often show random vertical leaps, perhaps signaling that the bobcat has jumped after a flying bird.

**Scat:** Tends to be constricted and, if dry, separates at constrictions into segments. Ends usually blunt. Dry scat falls apart. Scat from a fresh kill may form a cord of uniform diameter.

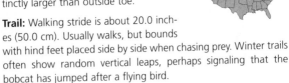

broken constriction

**scat**
3.0 x 0.8 in
7.5 x 2.0 cm

SCAT WIDTH

**Habitat:** Prefers dense cover of swamps and forests, especially with rocky ledges. Open agricultural land is not used. Rock piles, caves, and high rocky ledges are important for bearing young.

**Similar species:** Differs from coyote and other canids by lacking claws, having two lobes on the leading edge of the interdigital pad, and having toe 3 leading. Substantially smaller than both lion and lynx.

**Other sign:** Scent marks made by urine, scat, and anal glands. Scrapes dirt or snow over urine and scat. Scratches from rubbing glands are apparent on snow. Caches food by burying.

**walk**

**vertical leap from hind feet**

**bound**

**walk**

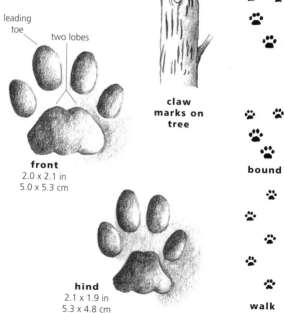

leading toe

two lobes

**front**
2.0 x 2.1 in
5.0 x 5.3 cm

**claw marks on tree**

**hind**
2.1 x 1.9 in
5.3 x 4.8 cm

*FRONT TRACK LENGTH*

*FRONT TRACK WIDTH*

# Canada Lynx
*Felis lynx*

Collie-size, with male averaging 22.0 pounds (10.0 kg) and female 19.0 pounds (9.0 kg). Very long legs and big feet. Reddish to yellowish brown overall, with dark spots or streaks and whitish underside. Ears have tufts at tips. Tail tip is black on top and bottom. Tail is short or bobbed, about 4.0 inches (10.0 cm) long.

**Track:** Diameter of a softball and indistinct because the feet are mostly covered with hair, and because pads are reduced in size. Feet are large, for better support on snow.

**Trail:** Walking stride is about 28.0 inches (70.0 cm). Walking gaits are common, but lynx does trot more than bobcat. Winter trails often show random vertical leaps, perhaps signalling that the lynx has jumped after a flying bird.

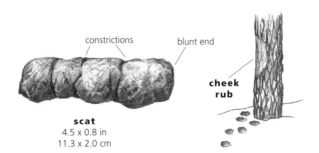

constrictions     blunt end

**cheek rub**

**scat**
4.5 x 0.8 in
11.3 x 2.0 cm

**Scat:** Tends to be constricted and, if dry, separates at constrictions into segments. Ends blunt. Dry scat falls apart. Scat from a fresh kill may form a cord of uniform diameter.

**Habitat:** Found in dense conifer forests interspersed with rocky ledges and downed timber, both of which are used for security and denning. Forest edges, which provide food for the lynx's major prey, snowshoe hare, are critical.

**Similar species:** Differs from other felids by being inherently indistinct. Interdigital pad is relatively small when compared to bobcat and mountain lion—check closely. Differs from canids by two lobes on interdigital pad and claws not showing.

**Other sign:** Birth dens occur in hollow logs, stumps, and clumps of timber. Adult lynx does not cover scat. Lynx urinates (scent marks) up to 25 times per mile. Sometimes rubs cheek on tree trunks.

fast trot

vertical
leap from
hind feet

trot

walk

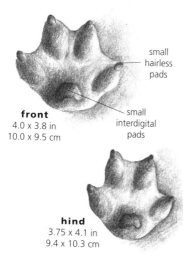

**front**
4.0 x 3.8 in
10.0 x 9.5 cm

small
hairless
pads

small
interdigital
pads

**hind**
3.75 x 4.1 in
9.4 x 10.3 cm

*FRONT TRACK LENGTH*

*FRONT TRACK WIDTH (50%)*

# Mountain Lion
*Puma concolor*

Larger than a German shepherd, with male averaging 145.0 pounds (66.0 kg) and female 120.0 pounds (54.0 kg). Color gray to red, often called tawny, with whitish underside. Back of ears and tail tip black to brown. Tail is more than half the length of the body. Also called cougar or puma.

**Track:** Track is diameter of a baseball. Front track round or wider than long, and hind track longer than wide. Claw impressions are usually absent. Toes form a slight arc, and toe 3 leads. Leading edge of the interdigital pad has two lobes. Inside toe distinctly larger.

**Trail:** Walking stride is about 36.0 inches (90.0 cm). Usually walks, but bounds with hind feet placed side by side when chasing prey.

**Scat:** Scat from a fresh kill may form a cord of uniform diameter with very slight constrictions; ends usually blunt. As the carcass on which a lion is feeding dries out, the lion's scat tends to develop constrictions, eventually falling apart when diet becomes very dry.

**scat**
4.0 x 1.25 in
10.0 x 3.1 cm

SCAT WIDTH

**Habitat:** Habitat is that of its main prey, deer. Open woodlands with rock ledges and grass (for deer) preferred. Often found in riparian zones with trees.

**Similar species:** Differs from wolf by the presence of two lobes on the leading edge of the interdigital pad, by having toe 3 leading, and by usually not showing claws. Differs from wolverine and bears by having only four toes and large toe inside.

**Other sign:** Often buries scat by scraping dirt over it with front feet. Scraped ground material may conceal food caches. Male will rake up basketball-size patches of brush and urinate on them to mark home range.

**Comments:** Breeding populations not known from area. Proof of nonferal or nonescaped animals is needed.

**bound**

**scraped ground around scat**

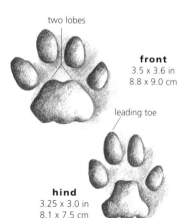

two lobes

**front**
3.5 x 3.6 in
8.8 x 9.0 cm

leading toe

**hind**
3.25 x 3.0 in
8.1 x 7.5 cm

**walk**

FRONT TRACK LENGTH

FRONT TRACK WIDTH

# Jaguar
*Panthera onca*

**Larger than a Doberman pincher, with weights usually 110.0 to 260.0 pounds (50.0 to 120.0 kg). Total length with tail may reach 8.0 feet (2.4 m). Skull appears large on body. Largest of North American cats. Females about 10 percent smaller. Color is buff to light gold with black rosettes; black jaguars do exist. Extremely rare in the United States.**

**Track:** Track larger than a softball. Front tracks round or wider than long, and hind tracks slightly longer than wide. Toes form a slight arc, and toe 3 leads. Leading edge of the interdigital pad has two lobes. Toes more rounded. Inside toe distinctly larger. Measurements are from two jaguars from Venezuela.

**Trail:** Walking stride is 40.0 to 55.0 inches (100.0 to 140.0 cm).

**Scat:** Uniform diameter cord with slight constrictions; ends usually blunt. When feeding on a dry diet, scat constricts and falls apart in short segments.

**scat**
6.4 x 1.5 in
16.0 x 3.8 cm

**Habitat:** In the United States found in dry, hilly country with rock outcroppings or cliffs interspersed with piñon pine–juniper vegetation. This may represent a marginal habitat, limiting northern extension of range.

**Similar species:** Track differs from mountain lion by having more broad, rounded tips on toes and its massive size. Tracks larger than all other felid species. Differ from those of canids by presence of two lobes on the anterior edge of the interdigital pad.

**Other sign:** Probably makes circular scrapes to mark by urination and probably covers scat in a similar manner to other felids.

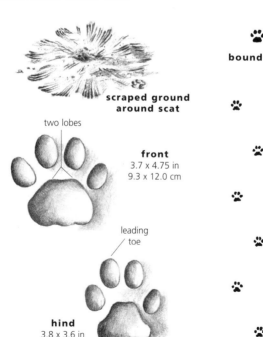

scraped ground
around scat

two lobes

**front**
3.7 x 4.75 in
9.3 x 12.0 cm

leading
toe

**hind**
3.8 x 3.6 in
9.5 x 9.0 cm

**bound**

**walk**

FRONT TRACK LENGTH

FRONT TRACK WIDTH (50%)

# Black Bear
*Ursus americanus*

Calf-size bear, female averaging 120.0 pounds (54.0 kg) and male 300.0 pounds (135.0 kg). Male grows faster and obtains larger size than female. Color varies from black to brown to blond to red. Special color phases, occasionally awarded subspecific status, include the white spirit or kermode bear (*U. a. kermode*) of British Columbia and the blue or glacier bear (*U. a. emmonsi*) of southern Alaska and British Columbia.

**Track:** Claws on front foot, seldom longer than toes, are usually present. Little toe is set back from rest of toes. Hind print has a large, humanlike heel. Outside toe is larger than others.

**Trail:** Walking stride 35.0 to 40.0 inches (88.0 to 100.0 cm). Usually ambles, a fast walk where the hind foot oversteps the front. Gait is pigeon-toed. Lopes in a C-shaped pattern or a side gallop.

**Scat:** Normally contains vegetation and is sweet-smelling. When

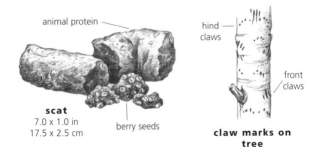

animal protein

**scat**
7.0 x 1.0 in
17.5 x 2.5 cm

berry seeds

hind claws

front claws

**claw marks on tree**

feeding on carcasses, scat varies from black to brown, with mostly hair and some bones. Ants often found in scat. Tips have a short taper or are blunt.

**Habitat:** Forest, seldom venturing far into wide openings. Thick understory vegetation and abundant food sources are critical.

**Similar species:** Differs from grizzly bear by smaller size, shorter claw length, and more curved arc of toes. Differs from wolverine by having toes tightly packed and having a wedge-shaped interdigital pad. Differs from lion and wolf by having five toes.

**Other sign:** Claws trees, rips open logs, digs into ant piles, and turns over rocks and scat as it looks for insects.

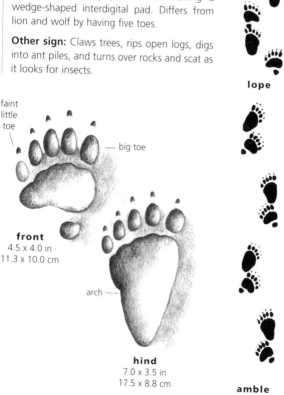

faint little toe

big toe

**front**
4.5 x 4.0 in
11.3 x 10.0 cm

arch

**hind**
7.0 x 3.5 in
17.5 x 8.8 cm

side lope

lope

amble

FRONT TRACK LENGTH

FRONT TRACK WIDTH (50%)

# Polar Bear
*Ursus maritimus*

Large bull-size bear, weighing up to about 1,800.0 pounds (820.0 kg). On average, the polar bear is the largest bear, although individual Kodiak bears compete in size. Color is

yellowish white in summer and winter but may be stained with dirt. Feeds almost exclusively on seals.

**Track:** Claws on front foot, typically as long as toes but curved and sharp. Webbing occurs between toes; look carefully. Hind print has a large, human-like heel. Outside toe larger than others.

**Trail:** Walking stride is 80.0 to 100.0 inches (200.0 to 250.0 cm). Usually ambles, a fast walk where the hind foot oversteps the front. Gait is pigeon-toed. Lopes in a C-shaped pattern or uses a side gallop.

**scat**
about 10.0 x 2.0 in
about 25.0 x 5.0 cm

SCAT WIDTH

**Scat:** During summer may contain remains of vegetation and berries. Most of the year contains remains of seals. Shells of blue mussels (*Mytilus edulis*) are found in fall scat when bears are waiting for the ocean pack ice to freeze.

**Habitat:** Coastal shores along the Arctic Ocean.

**Similar species:** Densely haired foot shows in footprints and separates polar bear tracks from other bears.

**Other sign:** Holes dug in kelp for beds or feeding. Appears to feed on the blue mussels in these kelp holes.

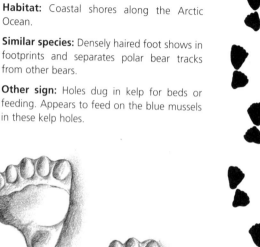

**front**
6.8 x 7.8 in
17.3 x 19.8 cm

**hind**
about 12.0 x 9.0 in
about 31.0 x 23.0 cm

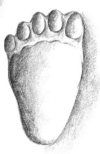

**amble**

# Kodiak and Coastal Brown Bears
*Ursus arctos middendorffi* and *U. a. dalli*

Kodiak bears may be bull-size, weighing up to about 1,500.0 pounds (680.0 kg). They are the largest brown bears and are found only on Kodiak and Afognak Islands.

Coastal brown bears may be cow-size, weighing up to about 1,200.0 pounds (550.0 kg). Color usually a shade of brown. All brown/grizzly bears are of the same species, *U. arctos*, but subspecific status is awarded by some authors; genetics studies suggest differences and hybridization. For tracking, differences in footprints are apparent. The Katmai and coastal brown bears are social bears used to feeding in congregations at salmon streams. They have small personal space into which humans are often welcome, allowing nearby viewing but with great care.

**Track:** Claws on front foot, typically more than 1.5 times longer than toes and blunt. Webbing occurs between toes; look carefully. Hind print has a large, humanlike heel. Outside toe larger than others.

**scat**
10.0 x 2.0 in
25.0 x 5.0 cm

SCAT WIDTH

**Trail:** Walking stride of Kodiak is 80.0 to 90.0 inches (200.0 to 230.0 cm) while coastal bear is 60.0 to 80.0 inches (150.0 to 200.0 cm). Usually ambles, a fast walk where the hind foot oversteps the front. Gait is pigeon-toed. Lopes in a C-shaped pattern or uses a side gallop.

**Scat:** Normally contains vegetation and is sweet-smelling. When feeding on salmon, scat may be a semiliquid mass with fish scales and fish odor. When feeding on berries, scat may be blue, but when feeding on grasses there is green texture.

**Habitat:** At the mouth of coastal streams, in berry patches, and grassy meadows.

**Similar species:** Differs from black bear by flatter arc of toes, longer claws, and webbing. Differs from grizzly bear by larger feet.

**Other sign:** Remains of salmon and wide trails beat down in the grass. Repeated use of trail leaves footprint holes as deep as 2.0 feet in the muskeg.

**side lope**

**lope**

**brown bear front**
5.1 x 5.7 in
13.0 x 14.3 cm

**Kodiak bear front:**
5.8 x 7.13 in
14.8 x 18.1 cm

**Kodiak bear hind:**
about 16.0 x 10.0 in
about 41.0 x 25.0 cm

**brown bear hind**
8.7 x 5.7 in
22.0 x 14.3

**amble**

*FRONT TRACK LENGTH (BROWN BEAR)*

*FRONT TRACK WIDTH (BROWN BEAR) (50%)*

# Grizzly Bear
*Ursus arctos horribilis*

Cow-size bear, female averaging 350.0 pounds (160.0 kg) and male 450.0 pounds (200.0 kg). Both sexes have hump over shoulders. Color varies from black to brown to blond. Light tips on individual hairs create the grizzled appearance for which grizzlies are named. All brown/grizzly bears are of the same species, *U. arctos*, but subspecific status is awarded by some authors; genetics studies suggest other differences and hybridization. For tracking, differences in footprints are apparent. The interior grizzly is a solitary bear with large personal space into which humans must tread lightly.

**Track:** Claws on front foot, typically more than 1.5 times longer than toes. Webbing occurs between toes; look carefully. Hind print has a large, human-like heel. Outside toe larger than others.

**Trail:** Walking stride is 50.0 to 60.0 inches (125.0 to 150.0 cm). Usually ambles, a fast walk where the hind foot

**scat**
7.0 x 1.5 in
17.5 x 3.8 cm

*SCAT WIDTH*

**trunk rub**

oversteps the front. Gait is pigeon-toed. Lopes in a C-shaped pattern or uses a side gallop.

**Scat:** Normally contains vegetation and is sweet-smelling. When feeding on carcasses, scat varies from black to brown, with mostly hair and some bones. When feeding in alpine areas may contain only parts of moths. Ants often found in scat. Tips have a short taper or are blunt.

**Habitat:** High forests to alpine tundra meadows. Stays close to cover, foraging at forest-meadow edge.

**Similar species:** Differs from black bear by flatter arc of toes, longer claws, and webbing. Differs from wolverine by having toes tightly packed and having a wedge-shaped interdigital pad. Differs from wolf and lion by having five toes.

**Other sign:** Claws trees, rips open logs, digs into ant piles, digs out roots and rodent caches, and turns over rocks and scat as it looks for insects. Rubs body against tree trunks, smoothing bark and leaving hair.

**side lope**

**lope**

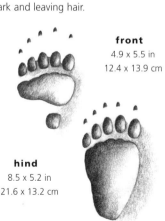

**front**
4.9 x 5.5 in
12.4 x 13.9 cm

**hind**
8.5 x 5.2 in
21.6 x 13.2 cm

**amble**

*FRONT TRACK LENGTH*

*FRONT TRACK WIDTH (50%)*

# Ringtail
*Bassariscus astutus*

Small, rat-size, with a bushy tail as long as its body. Males average 1.5 to 2.5 pounds (0.7 to 1.1 kg), with females slightly smaller. Pointed face, large eyes and ears. Tan to gray overall, with some black hairs. Tail has black bands alternating with white to a black tip.

**Track:** Five toes, round and somewhat bulbous, with a proximal pad showing in the front print. Claws are semi-retractile and may not show.

**Trail:** Bounding stride is 12 to 16 inches (30 to 40 cm). Uses a relatively slow bound or lope much of the time.

**Scat:** Usually composed of plant material, but occasionally black animal protein scats are found. Insects and fruits are often present.

**Habitat:** Found in a variety of habitats from riparian to desert to open woodland to evergreen forest. Rest sites and dens are

**scat**
2.0 x 0.4 in
5.0 x 1.0 cm

**chewed cactus on cliff runway**

SCAT WIDTH

located in rocks, burrows, brushpiles, and hollow limbs. Not averse to using buildings for nests and dens.

**Similar species:** Differs from domestic cats, bobcats, and small foxes by having five toes and a proximal pad.

**Other sign:** Runways at the bases of cliffs are used repeatedly, and trails often lead to a single rock crevice where it dens.

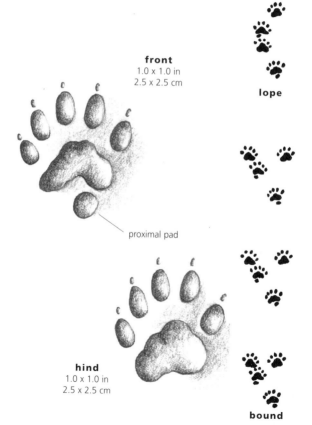

**front**
1.0 x 1.0 in
2.5 x 2.5 cm

proximal pad

**hind**
1.0 x 1.0 in
2.5 x 2.5 cm

**lope**

**bound**

FRONT TRACK LENGTH

FRONT TRACK WIDTH

# Coati
*Nasua narica*

Larger than a border collie, weighing 15.0 to 25.0 pounds (7.0 to 11.0 kg). Distinguished by long tail and long snout. Considerable body color variation ranging from pale reddish brown to almost black and interspersed with yellows. Dark mask on face and yellowish or brown rings on tail. Rings may be faint to nearly nonexistent.

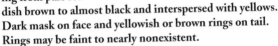

**Track:** Five toes on front and hind tracks. Toes are slightly bulbous at tips. Hind track shows a long, naked heel that may not register on a hard surface. Claw length equals or exceeds toe length.

**Trail:** Walking stride is 14.0 inches (36.0 cm). Generally a rambling trail investigating many objects.

**scat**
2.8 x 0.6 in
7.0 x 1.5 cm

SCAT WIDTH

**Scat:** Highly variable depending on the diet. Often a black, even-diameter cord with blunt ends.

**Habitat:** Prefers chaparral to open dry deciduous forests.

**Similar species:** Differs from raccoon by presence of long claws and relatively less bulbous toe tips.

**Other sign:** Disturbs ground litter by rooting as it looks for insects and grubs.

**front**
2.4 x 1.8 in
6.0 x 4.5 cm

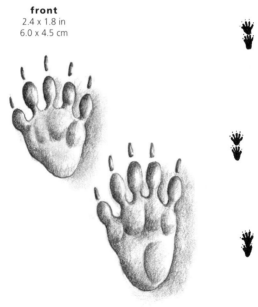

**hind**
2.8 x 1.8 in
7.0 x 4.5 cm

**slow walk**

FRONT TRACK LENGTH

FRONT TRACK WIDTH

# Raccoon
*Procyon lotor*

Stocky, smaller
than a border col-
lie, with broad head
and bushy tail. Male
averages 18.0 pounds
(8.0 kg) and female
16.0 pounds (7.0 kg).
Gray to black overall, with black rings on the tail and a black
mask on a white face.

**Track:** Five slender toes, slightly bulbous on the ends. Feet resemble
small human hands and feet. Hind
foot has a long, naked heel.

**Trail:** Walking stride averages 27.0
inches (68.0 cm). Roll of hips during
walk causes hind foot to register
beside the opposite front print.
C-shaped gallop is common.

**Scat:** Highly variable, but often black, even-diameter cord with
blunt ends. Often contains crayfish or fruit. Deposited singly or in
dung heaps containing scat from perhaps several raccoons. **May
carry a parasite that is fatal to humans. Do not smell scat,
and wash hands after touching.**

**Habitat:** River and stream drainages are prime habitats, but storm
drains in cities may also provide refuge. Woodpiles in and around
towns.

**scat**
3.0 x 0.75 in
7.5 x 1.9 cm

SCAT WIDTH

**Similar species:** Differs from bear in having slender toes. Differs from river otter by lack of webbing. Larger than mink.

**Other sign:** Digs holes in streambanks to get at crayfish. Leaves piles of crayfish exoskeletons and claws. Digs for worms in lawns.

**sign left while fishing for crayfish**

bulbous toe

narrow neck

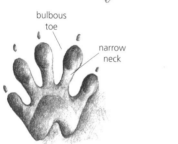

**front**
2.5 x 2.5 in
6.3 x 6.3 cm

**gallop**

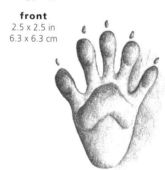

**hind**
4.0 x 2.3 in
10.0 x 5.8 cm

**walk**

FRONT TRACK LENGTH

FRONT TRACK WIDTH

# Long-tailed Weasel
*Mustela frenata*

Slender-bodied
carnivore about
the size of a
foot-long hot dog
(13.0 inches/32.5 cm,
without tail). Pointed, flat skull with small ears. Males about
1.0 pound (0.5 kg). Male up to twice as large as female.
Overall color is brown, with a white belly. Hairy, slender tail
with black tip. In winter, northern individuals turn entirely
white.

**Track:** Wide track. Five toes, in 1-3-1 grouping. Little toe, on
inside of foot, often does not register.
Interdigital pad chevron-shaped. Heel
seldom shows. Difficult to distinguish
among species.

**Trail:** Galloping stride varies from 8.0 to
30.0 inches (20.0 to 75.0 cm). Side-by-
side tracks, when examined closely, show
one track slightly in front of the other—a
gallop. In snow, a drag mark may be
found between front and hind prints,
sometimes forming a dumbbell shape.

**Scat:** Long, slender cord, usually with black, toothpastelike animal protein or hair. Cord tends to fold back on itself. Tapered at
both ends.

folded back ──────

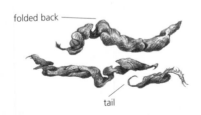

**scat**
1.5 x 0.1 in
3.8 x 0.3 cm

tail

SCAT WIDTH

**Habitat:** Prefers dense, low ground cover to open areas. Found in habitats where their prey, rodents, occur in high densities. Trails often lead from one rodent den to another. Travels in snow and ground burrows of other mammals.

**Similar species:** Differs from other mustelids by their smaller size and the drag mark commonly located between twin track patterns in the snow.

**Other sign:** Routes seldom follow a straight line, often having many sharp turns. Scat often deposited on raised objects.

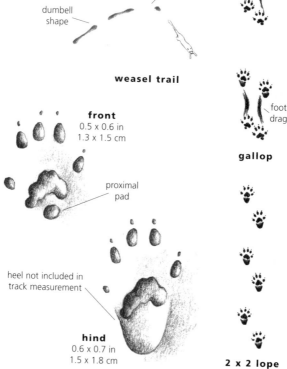

erratic route

dumbell shape

**weasel trail**

**front**
0.5 x 0.6 in
1.3 x 1.5 cm

proximal pad

heel not included in track measurement

**hind**
0.6 x 0.7 in
1.5 x 1.8 cm

foot drag

**gallop**

**2 x 2 lope**

*FRONT TRACK LENGTH*

*FRONT TRACK WIDTH*

# Marten
*Martes americana*

Size of a small
domestic cat, but
slender, 1.0 to
4.0 pounds (0.5 to
1.8 kg). Male 20 per-
cent larger than female.
Pointed, flat skull with small ears.
Overall color golden brown, with orange to yellow chest
patch. Edges of ears are white. Hairy, slender tail.

**Track:** Five toes, in 1-3-1 grouping. Little
toe, on the inside of foot, sometimes does
not register. Interdigital pad is a chevron.
Proximal pad may show in front footprint.
Heel often shows. Feet are well furred in
winter, making tracks indistinct.

**Trail:** Gallop stride averages 22.0 inches
(55.0 cm). Mostly gallops; a variety of
2 x 2, 3 x 3, and 4 x 4 patterns will be
found.

**Scat:** Long, slender cord, tending to fold back on itself. Black or
brown in color, occasionally with hair. Tapered at both ends.

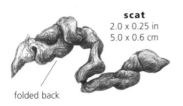

**scat**
2.0 x 0.25 in
5.0 x 0.6 cm

folded back

**climbs tree,
jumps out**

SCAT WIDTH

**Habitat:** Old-growth forest, but adaptable to many forest habitats. Prefers mature conifer and mixed forests. Needs tall, hollow, or broken trees for denning. Found near its prey, squirrels and red-backed voles.

**Similar species:** Differs from weasel by its larger size. Lacks the webbed toes of the mink. Also differs from mink by use of terrestrial habitat. Smaller than fisher and occupies areas with deeper snow.

**Other sign:** Frequently burrows beneath snow and climbs up trees; look for tracks that end at a tree trunk. Scratch marks show where stomach was dragged over objects that protrude from the ground or snow to scent mark.

**4 x 4 gallop**

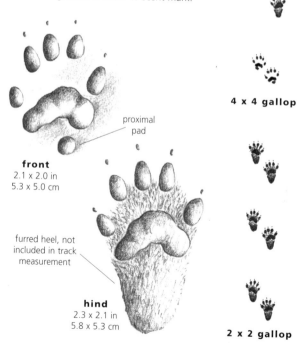

proximal pad

**front**
2.1 x 2.0 in
5.3 x 5.0 cm

furred heel, not included in track measurement

**hind**
2.3 x 2.1 in
5.8 x 5.3 cm

**2 x 2 gallop**

*FRONT TRACK LENGTH*

*FRONT TRACK WIDTH*

# Mink
*Mustela vison*

Size of a small
domestic cat, but
slender, 1.5 to 3.5
pounds (0.7 to 1.5 kg).
Male 10 percent larger
than female. Pointed, flat skull with small
ears. Overall color is dark brown, with white
spots on chin and chest. Hairy, slender tail. Webbing occurs
between the toes.

**Track:** Five toes, in 1-3-1 grouping. Little toe, on the inside of foot, sometimes does not register. Webbing shows between toes in tracks; look carefully. Interdigital pad chevron-shaped. Proximal pad may show in front footprint. Heel seldom shows.

**Trail:** Bounding stride averages 14.0 inches (35.0 cm). Bounds more than weasels, but a gallop, averaging 20.0 inches (50.0 cm), is also common.

**Scat:** Long, slender cord, usually tending to fold back on itself. Black or brown in color, occasionally with hair. Tapered at both ends. Often contains remains of fish or crayfish. May be oily and smell fishy. Fish oil keeps scat composed of fish scales from falling apart until oil evaporates, then scales scatter on the ground.

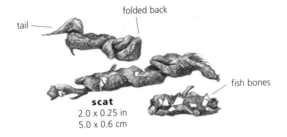

tail — folded back

fish bones

**scat**
2.0 x 0.25 in
5.0 x 0.6 cm

SCAT WIDTH

**Habitat:** River- and streambanks. Seldom far from water.

**Similar species:** Differs from other small mustelids by having more webbing between toes. Larger than weasels. Use of aquatic habitat is an important clue for separation from marten. Tracks and trail much smaller than those of otter.

**Other sign:** Mink make "post offices," repeated scat deposits on logs exposed above water's edge. Strong, musky, almost skunklike odor from anal scent glands.

**fast walk**

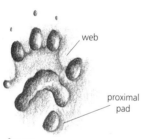

web

proximal pad

**front**
1.7 x 1.8 in
4.3 x 4.5 cm

web

**hind**
1.8 x 1.9 in
4.5 x 4.8 cm

**bound**

FRONT TRACK LENGTH

FRONT TRACK WIDTH

# Black-footed Ferret
*Mustela nigripes*

Long and slen-
der, twice the
size of a weasel,
1.4 to 3.0
pounds (0.6 to
1.4 kg). Pointed, flat skull with small ears. Overall color pale
yellow-brown, with dark hairs on back. Black mask across
the eyes. Black feet and tail tip. Hairy, slender tail.

**Track:** Five toes, in 1-3-1 grouping. Little
toe, on the inside of foot, sometimes does
not register. Interdigital pad is a chevron.
Proximal pad may show in front footprint.
Heel may show. Claws may not show.

**Trail:** Galloping and bounding strides average 20.0 inches (50.0 cm). Bounds more
than weasels, but a gallop is very common.

**Scat:** Long, slender cord, usually with
black, toothpastelike animal protein or hair. Cord tends to fold
back on itself. Tapered at both ends.

**Habitat:** Found in prairie dog towns in native short-grass prairies
(prairie dogs are their main food).

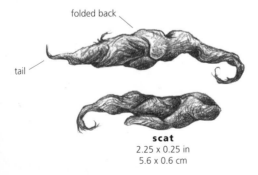

folded back

tail

**scat**
2.25 x 0.25 in
5.6 x 0.6 cm

SCAT WIDTH

**Similar species:** Differs from weasel by larger track and trail. Differs from mink and marten by (sometimes) being larger. Mink and marten are seldom found in prairie dog towns.

**Other sign:** Excavated subsoil trough extending 40.0 to 55.0 inches (100.0 to 140.0 cm) from prairie dog mounds.

**3 x 3 gallop**

**trough**

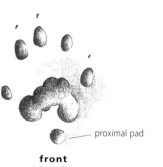

proximal pad

**front**
1.2 x 1.3 in
3.0 x 3.3 cm

**4 x 4 gallop**

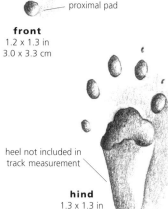

heel not included in
track measurement

**hind**
1.3 x 1.3 in
3.3 x 3.3 cm

**2 x 2 bound**

FRONT TRACK LENGTH

FRONT TRACK WIDTH

# Fisher
*Martes pennanti*

Larger than a
large domestic
cat, but slender,
7.5 to 12.0 pounds
(3.0 to 5.0 kg). Male
larger than female.
Pointed, flat skull with small ears. Color is dark brown. Long
bushy tail.

**Track:** Five toes, in 1-3-1 grouping. Little toe, on the inside of foot, sometimes does not register. Interdigital pad chevron-shaped. Proximal pad may show in front footprint. Heel seldom shows. Claws short. Feet are not well furred, which, in winter, makes toes appear clearly in tracks.

**Trail:** Galloping stride averages 28.0 inches (70.0 cm). Mostly gallops, but walking, 3 x 3, 1 x 2 x 1, and 4 x 4 gallop patterns are also common.

**Scat:** Only mustelid scat that frequently contains porcupine quills. Long, slender cord, usually tending to fold back on itself. Black or brown in color, occasionally with hair. Tapered at both ends.

**Habitat:** Old-growth forest, especially among conifers and large timber, and in swamp areas. Upland hardwood stands where porcupines den. Will use young forest stands following fire or timber

folded back

tail

**scat**
3.5 x 0.5 in
8.8 x 1.3 cm

SCAT WIDTH

harvest. Avoids open areas without overhead cover, but will travel on roads and trails.

**Similar species:** Lacks the webbed toes of the mink. Differs from mink by habitat and use of terrestrial sites. Larger than mink and marten and occupies areas of shallower snow. Smaller than wolverine and makes more frequent use of trees for walkways and nests.

**Other sign:** Porcupine skins turned inside out. Snow trails may reveal frequent trips up trees. Walks on logs to avoid deep snow. Drags stomach over objects that protrude from the ground or snow to scent mark, leaving scratches. Travels on packed trails of snowshoe hare.

**1 x 2 x 1
lope**

**3 x 3 lope**

**2 x 2 gallop**

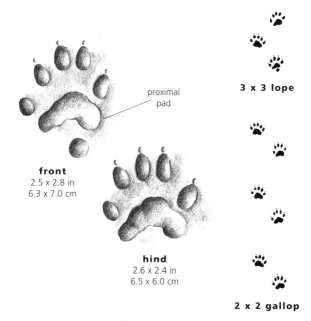

**front**
2.5 x 2.8 in
6.3 x 7.0 cm

proximal
pad

**hind**
2.6 x 2.4 in
6.5 x 6.0 cm

FRONT TRACK LENGTH

FRONT TRACK WIDTH

# River Otter
*Lutra canadensis*

Body and tail form a
4.0-foot-long cylin-
der that tapers to a
hairy, pointed tail. Weight
varies from 10.0 to 30.0 pounds
(5.0 to 14.0 kg). Male slightly larger than
female. Overall color a rich, dark brown,
with silver-brown belly. Webbed toes on front and hind feet.

**Track:** Large webbed foot is diagnostic, but look closely because
webbing may be difficult to see.
Hind foot is very wide. Five toes, in
1-3-1 grouping. Little toe, on the
inside of foot, sometimes does not
register. Interdigital pad chevron-
shaped. Proximal pad often shows.
Hairless heel on hind foot.

**Trail:** Walking stride averages 19.0 inches (48.0 cm). Loping stride
averages 32.0 inches (80.0 cm). Loping gait patterns are usually
turned to the side.

**Scat:** Usually contains fish remains, including scales and verte-
brae. The texture is oily and the smell fishy. Fish oil keeps scat
composed of fish scales from falling apart. Scat decomposes as oil
evaporates, eventually falling into a pile of scales.

fish parts

**scat**
5.0 x 1.0 in
12.5 x 2.5 cm

SCAT WIDTH

**Habitat:** River- and streambeds. Lives and nests in bank burrows, but may also nest in log jams. In spring, travels overland, often several miles from water sources.

**Similar species:** Differs from other species by webbing and large, wide hind foot.

**Other sign:** Loose dirt banks show where otters have rolled to dry off. Rolls around tufts of grass, twisting them into scent posts. Travels by sliding down banks and along level snow and over ice-covered lakes.

**tail drag**

**side lope**

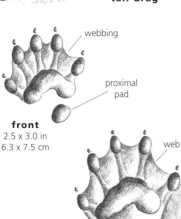

webbing

proximal pad

**front**
2.5 x 3.0 in
6.3 x 7.5 cm

web

**hind**
3.0 x 3.6 in
7.5 x 9.0 cm

**bound**

FRONT TRACK LENGTH

FRONT TRACK WIDTH

# Wolverine
*Gulo gulo*

**Body like a badger's, but heavier, up to 35.0 pounds (16.0 kg). Male larger than female. Head broad, rounded, and flat. Color varies from overall dark brown with light blond side stripes to nearly all blond. Short tail.**

**Track:** Track diameter of a baseball. Five toes, in 1-3-1 grouping. Little toe, on the inside of foot, sometimes does not register. Interdigital pad is a chevron. Proximal pad and heel often show. Distinct winter tracks because feet are not well furred.

**Trail:** Gallop stride averages 35.0 inches (90.0 cm). Mostly 2 x 2 and 3 x 3 gallop patterns.

**Scat:** Long, medium-diameter cord occasionally folding back on itself. Black or brown, occasionally with hair. Tapered at both ends. Similar to large coyote scat.

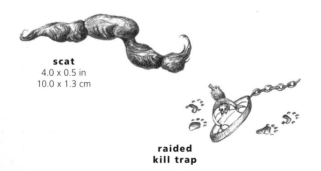

**scat**
4.0 x 0.5 in
10.0 x 1.3 cm

**raided
kill trap**

SCAT WIDTH

**Habitat:** Not habitat-specific. Wanders widely in all seasons, though often found where there are wintering deer, elk, or moose.

**Similar species:** Larger than mink, marten, and fisher, and only rarely climbs trees. Differs from wolf and lion by having five toes. Differs from bear by having 1-3-1 toe grouping and chevron-shaped interdigital pad.

**Other sign:** Scavenges on old carcasses, including animals caught in kill traps. Revisits sites to dig carcasses from under snow. Drags stomach over objects that protrude from ground or snow to scent mark, leaving scratches. Trails cross large openings in trees and are often found above tree line. Travels on packed trails and roads.

**3 x 3
gallop**

**1 x 2 x 1
lope**

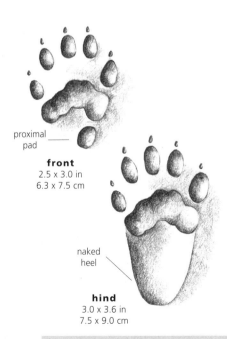

proximal pad

**front**
2.5 x 3.0 in
6.3 x 7.5 cm

naked heel

**hind**
3.0 x 3.6 in
7.5 x 9.0 cm

*FRONT TRACK LENGTH*

*FRONT TRACK WIDTH*

# Badger

*Taxidea taxus*

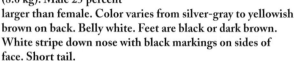

Border collie–size, with flat body, long hair, and long, shovel-like claws, about 18.0 pounds (8.0 kg). Male 25 percent larger than female. Color varies from silver-gray to yellowish brown on back. Belly white. Feet are black or dark brown. White stripe down nose with black markings on sides of face. Short tail.

**Track:** Diameter of a golf ball, with long front claws, nearly as long as rest of footprint. Five toes, in 1-3-1 grouping. Little toe, on the inside of foot, sometimes does not register. Interdigital pad chevron-shaped. Proximal pad often shows. Front footprint larger than hind.

**Trail:** Walking stride averages 14.0 inches (35.0 cm). Walking is most common, but trotting, with a stride of 29.0 inches (74.0 cm), occurs frequently.

**Scat:** Seldom found because deposited below ground in burrows. Similar to, but smaller than, coyote scat, without tapered ends.

**scat**
3.0 x 0.8 in
7.5 x 2.0 cm

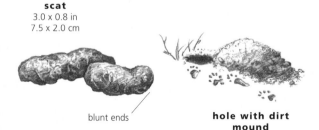

blunt ends

**hole with dirt mound**

**Habitat:** Open grasslands preferred. Areas with large populations of prey, which includes ground squirrels and prairie dogs.

**Similar species:** Differs from all other species by long claws on front foot and disproportionately small hind foot.

**Other sign:** Fresh excavations of large amounts of dirt from burrowing rodent holes indicates hunting activity, especially if excavated material includes large clods or rocks. Freshly widened burrow entrances may have a slightly elliptical shape. The presence of coyote and badger tracks together indicates cooperative hunting.

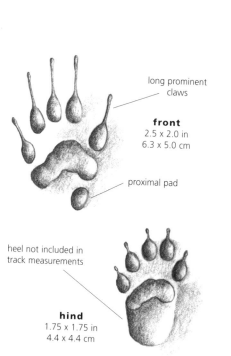

long prominent claws

**front**
2.5 x 2.0 in
6.3 x 5.0 cm

**1 x 2 x 1
lope**

proximal pad

heel not included in track measurements

**hind**
1.75 x 1.75 in
4.4 x 4.4 cm

**walk**

FRONT TRACK LENGTH

FRONT TRACK WIDTH

# Striped Skunk
*Mephitis mephitis*

Black-and-white mustelid, size of a domestic cat, with triangular head. Weight varies from 4.0 to 10.0 pounds (2.0 to 5.0 kg). Male is slightly larger than female. Flat, wide, bushy tail with white hair on top. Long, curved claws for digging.

**Track:** Half dollar–size, with long front claws. Hind track looks like a little human footprint. Five toes, in 1-3-1 grouping. Little toe, on the inside of foot, sometimes does not register. Interdigital pad chevron-shaped. Proximal pad often shows. Hairless heel on hind foot.

**Trail:** Walking stride averages 12.0 inches (30.0 cm). Meanders and stops often when walking, leaving extra footprints in trail. Lope may be turned to the side or straight forward.

**Scat:** Cylindrical with blunt ends. Lacks the long taper and tendency to fold back on itself of other mustelid scat. May be composed entirely of insect parts.

blunt

**scat**
5.0 x 0.75 in
12.5 x 1.9 cm

fanged puncture

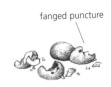

**chewed eggs**

**Habitat:** Not habitat-specific. Lives where burrows, cavities, or tunnels are present, including in and around buildings. Presence of insects and small mammals is critical to habitat selection.

**Similar species:** Differs from other species by having long, wide claws on the front foot. Smaller than badger, with front and hind feet similar in size.

**Other sign:** Smell of skunk musk identifies nests and burrows. Tears apart nests of small mammals. Bird eggs show four fang punctures around larger hole in shell.

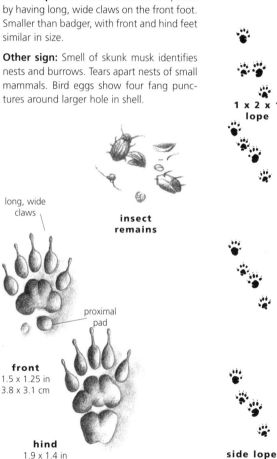

insect
remains

long, wide
claws

proximal
pad

**front**
1.5 x 1.25 in
3.8 x 3.1 cm

**hind**
1.9 x 1.4 in
4.8 x 3.5 cm

**1 x 2 x 1
lope**

**side lope**

FRONT TRACK LENGTH

FRONT TRACK WIDTH

# Spotted Skunk
*Spilogale putorius*

**Black-and-white mustelid, size of a small domestic cat. Male weighs 1.0 to 2.0 pounds (0.5 to 0.9 kg), female 0.5 to 1.25 pounds (0.25 to 0.6 kg). Distinctive pattern of white spot on forehead, a spot by each ear, four white stripes along each side, and a white tip on tail. Spots and stripes highly variable.**

**Track:** Size of a quarter, with longer claws on front footprint. Five toes, though 1-3-1 grouping is difficult to identify. Little toe, on the inside of foot, may not register. Clear front and hind prints on a hard surface may show a total of six hairless interdigital and proximal pads. Plantigrade heel on hind foot.

**Trail:** Loping stride is about 12.0 inches (30.0 cm). Short bounds are very common. Often rambles as it walks, leaving a confused trail with most front and hind prints registering separately.

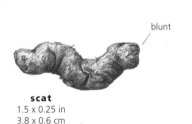

blunt

**scat**
1.5 x 0.25 in
3.8 x 0.6 cm

SCAT WIDTH

**insect remains**

**Scat:** Cylindrical, with blunt ends. Lacks the long taper and tendency to fold back on itself of other mustelid scat. May include mouse fur, bird feathers, insects, and carrion.

**Habitat:** Brush, chaparral, and open woodlands, especially along streams and in boulder areas.

**Similar species:** Distinguished from striped skunk by smaller track size and multiple foot pads.

**Other sign:** Nests in burrows beneath rock- and woodpiles or under buildings.

lope

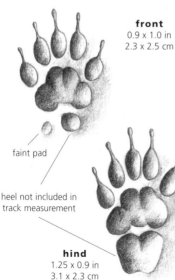

**front**
0.9 x 1.0 in
2.3 x 2.5 cm

faint pad

heel not included in
track measurement

**hind**
1.25 x 0.9 in
3.1 x 2.3 cm

side lope

# Eastern Cottontail Rabbit

*Sylvilagus floridanus*

Small rabbit with large ears and feet, small white tail. Averages 3.0 pounds (1.4 kg). Color pepper-and-salt or gray and white. Several species of cottontail are found in North America. Their tracks are difficult to distinguish from one another. Tracks and scat may vary only slightly in size among species.

**Track:** Toes asymmetrical around foot axis. Track indistinct because the foot is completely haired and lacks pads. Occasionally claws will register; these may be the only sign of a hopping rabbit. Hind footprint about two and a half times longer than front.

**Trail:** Hopping stride is about 3.0 feet (90.0 cm). Most of the time rabbits hop, but walking patterns will occasionally be observed.

**Scat:** Dry scat is a slightly flattened sphere. Produces a black, semi-liquid scat that is usually reingested to utilize remaining nutrients.

**scat**
0.3 in
0.8 cm

**chewed branch and bud**

SCAT WIDTH

**Habitat:** Found wherever there is grass for food and suitable cover, including brushpiles, herbaceous and shrubby vegetation, and grasslands. May use dens of other animals for escape cover.

**Similar species:** Differs from jackrabbit and hare by having shorter heels and smaller overall size.

**Other sign:** Sharp incisors cleanly cut herbaceous vegetation at the height of a sitting rabbit, 4.0 to 8.0 inches (10.0 to 20.0 cm). Look for tips of branches with young sprouts chewed off. The cottontail's nest, known as a *form,* is a shallow depression in earth, grass, or snow.

**walk**

**claws only
on hard
ground**

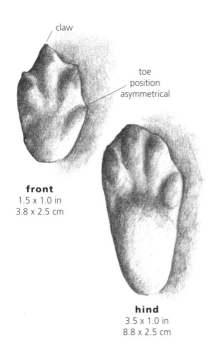

claw

toe
position
asymmetrical

**front**
1.5 x 1.0 in
3.8 x 2.5 cm

**hind**
3.5 x 1.0 in
8.8 x 2.5 cm

**hop**

*FRONT TRACK LENGTH*

*FRONT TRACK WIDTH*

# Mountain Cottontail Rabbit
*Sylvilagus nuttallii*

**Small rabbit with large ears and feet, small white tail. Averages 1.0 pound (0.5 kg). Color pepper-and-salt or gray and white. Several species of cottontail are found in North America. Their tracks are difficult to distinguish from one another. Tracks and scat may vary only slightly in size among species.**

**Track:** Toes asymmetrical around foot axis. Track indistinct because the foot is completely haired and lacks pads. Occasionally claws will register; these may be the only sign of a hopping rabbit. Hind footprint about two and a half times longer than front.

**Trail:** Hopping stride is about 3.0 feet (90.0 cm). Most of the time rabbits hop, but walking patterns will occasionally be observed.

**Scat:** Dry scat is a slightly flattened sphere. Produces a black, semi-liquid scat that is usually reingested to utilize remaining nutrients.

**scat**
0.2 in
0.5 cm

SCAT WIDTH

**chewed branch and bud**

**Habitat:** Found wherever there is grass for food and suitable cover, including brushpiles, herbaceous and shrubby vegetation, and grasslands. May use dens of other animals for escape cover.

**Similar species:** Differs from jackrabbit and hare by having shorter heels and smaller overall size.

**Other sign:** Sharp incisors cleanly cut herbaceous vegetation at the height of a sitting rabbit 4.0 to 8.0 inches (10.0 to 20.0 cm). Look for tips of branches with young sprouts chewed off. The cottontail's nest, known as a *form*, is a shallow depression in earth, grass, or snow.

**walk**

**claws only on hard ground**

claw

toe position asymmetrical

**front**
1.25 x 1.0 in
3.2 x 2.5 cm

**hind**
2.0 x 1.0 in
5.0 x 2.5 cm

**hop**

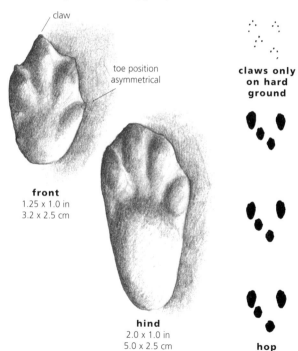

FRONT TRACK LENGTH

FRONT TRACK WIDTH

# Brush Cottontail
*Sylvilagus bachmani*

Small cottontail rabbit with relatively short ears; weighs
about 1.5 pounds (675.0 g).
Body is brownish, with a
small white tuft of tail.
Several species of cottontail are found in North
America. Their tracks are
difficult to distinguish
from one another. Tracks
and scat may vary only slightly in
size among species.

**Track:** Toes asymmetrical around foot
axis. Track indistinct because the foot
is completely haired and lacks pads.
Claws occasionally register; on hard
ground, they may be the only sign of a
hopping rabbit. Hind footprint about
two and a half times as long as front.

**Trail:** Hopping stride is about 36.0 inches (90.0 cm). Most of the
time rabbits hop, but walking patterns are occasionally
observed.

SCAT WIDTH

**scat**
0.2 in
0.5 cm

**chewed
branch
and bud**

**Scat:** Dry scat is a slightly flattened sphere. Produces a black, semiliquid scat that is usually reingested to utilize remaining nutrients.

**Habitat:** Thick brush and chaparral interspersed with grass.

**Similar species:** Differs from jackrabbit and hare by having shorter heels and smaller overall size.

**Other sign:** Sharp incisors cut herbaceous vegetation at the height of a sitting rabbit, 4.0 to 6.0 inches (10.0 to 15.0 cm). The cottontail's nest, known as a *form,* is a shallow depression in earth or grass.

**claws only on hard ground**

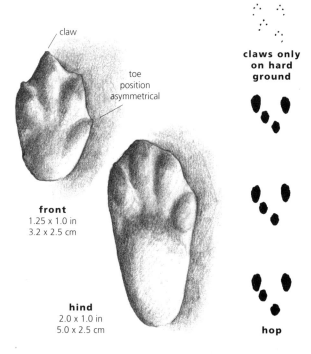

claw

toe position asymmetrical

**front**
1.25 x 1.0 in
3.2 x 2.5 cm

**hind**
2.0 x 1.0 in
5.0 x 2.5 cm

**hop**

FRONT TRACK LENGTH

FRONT TRACK WIDTH

# Desert Cottontail
*Sylvilagus auduboni*

Medium-size rabbit with large ears; weighs about 2.0 pounds (0.9 kg). Body is gray and yellow, with a small white tuft of tail. Several species of cottontail are found in North America. Their tracks are difficult to distinguish from one another. Tracks and scat may vary only slightly in size among species.

**Track:** Toes asymmetrical around foot axis. Track indistinct because the foot is completely haired and lacks pads. Occasionally claws will register; these may be the only sign of a hopping rabbit. Hind footprint about two times longer than front.

**Trail:** Hopping stride is about 36.0 inches (90.0 cm). Most of the time rabbits hop, but walking patterns will occasionally be observed.

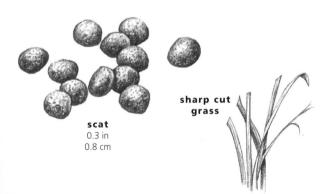

**scat**
0.3 in
0.8 cm

**sharp cut grass**

SCAT WIDTH

**Scat:** Dry scat is a slightly flattened sphere. Produces a black, semiliquid scat usually reingested to utilize remaining nutrients.

**Habitat:** Thick brush and chaparral interspersed with grass.

**Similar species:** Differs from jackrabbit and hare by having shorter heels and smaller overall size.

**Other sign:** Sharp incisors cleanly cut herbaceous vegetation at the height of a sitting rabbit, 4.0 to 6.0 inches (10.0 to 20.0 cm). The cottontail's nest, known as a *form,* is a shallow depression in earth or grass.

**walk**

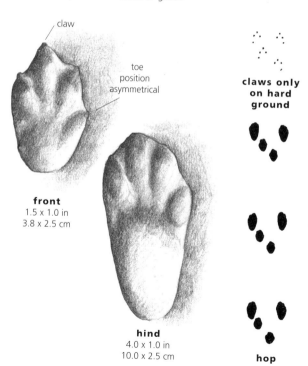

claw

toe position asymmetrical

**front**
1.5 x 1.0 in
3.8 x 2.5 cm

**hind**
4.0 x 1.0 in
10.0 x 2.5 cm

**claws only on hard ground**

**hop**

FRONT TRACK LENGTH

FRONT TRACK WIDTH

# Black-tailed Jackrabbit
*Lepus californicus*

Large, slender hare with long (6.0 inches/15.0 cm) ears and large feet. Weighs 3.0 to 7.0 pounds (1.4 to 3.2 kg). Body color is brownish gray. Tips of ears, top of tail, and rump are black.

**Track:** Toes asymmetrical around foot axis. Track indistinct because the foot is completely haired and lacks pads. Claws occasionally register; on hard ground, they may be the only sign of a footprint. Hind footprint about three times longer than front. Footprints of white-tailed jackrabbit are about 10 percent longer.

**Trail:** Galloping stride may reach 10.0 feet (3.0 m). Tends to gallop rather than bound.

**scat**
0.3 in
0.8 cm

**sharp cut grass**

SCAT WIDTH

**Scat:** Dry scat is a slightly flattened sphere. Produces a black, semiliquid scat that is usually reingested to utilize remaining nutrients.

**Habitat:** Sparsely vegetated open areas of the desert and plains.

**Similar species:** Hind track differs from cottontail by greater length. May not be possible to tell from white-tailed jackrabbit.

**Other sign:** Sharp incisors cleanly cut herbaceous vegetation at the height of a sitting rabbit, 4.0 to 6.0 inches (10.0 to 15.0 cm). The jackrabbit's nest, known as a *form*, is a shallow depression, usually located under protective cover.

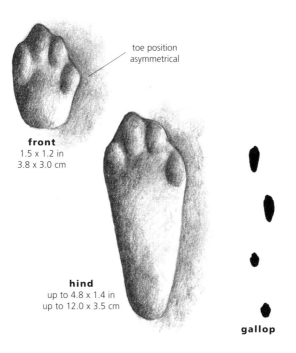

toe position asymmetrical

**front**
1.5 x 1.2 in
3.8 x 3.0 cm

**hind**
up to 4.8 x 1.4 in
up to 12.0 x 3.5 cm

**gallop**

FRONT TRACK LENGTH

FRONT TRACK WIDTH

# White-tailed Jackrabbit

*Lepus townsendii*

**Large, slender hare with long ears and feet. Averages 5.0 pounds (2.0 kg). Body color is gray and white to black and white, with white tail. May turn white in winter.**

**Track:** Toes asymmetrical around foot axis. Track indistinct because foot is completely haired and lacks pads. Occasionally claws will register, and may be the only sign of a footprint. Hind footprint may be up to three times longer than front. Hind print of white-tailed jackrabbit averages 10 percent longer than black-tailed.

**Trail:** Galloping stride may reach 10.0 feet (3.0 m). Tends to gallop rather than bound.

**scat**
0.3 in
0.8 cm

SCAT WIDTH

**sharp cut grass**

**Scat:** Dry scat is a slightly flattened sphere. Produces a black, semiliquid scat that is usually reingested to utilize remaining nutrients.

**Habitat:** Inhabits open areas. Found from plains grasslands to above tree line in mountains.

**Similar species:** Differs from cottontail by greater length. Differs from snowshoe hare by its narrow width.

**Other sign:** Sharp incisors cleanly cut herbaceous and woody vegetation. The jackrabbit's nest, known as a *form,* is a shallow depression, usually found under protective cover.

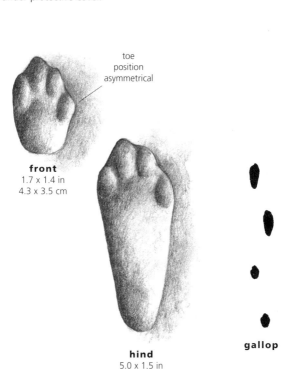

toe position asymmetrical

**front**
1.7 x 1.4 in
4.3 x 3.5 cm

**hind**
5.0 x 1.5 in
12.5 x 3.8 cm

**gallop**

FRONT TRACK LENGTH

FRONT TRACK WIDTH

# Snowshoe Hare
*Lepus americanus*

**Medium-size hare with long ears and feet. Averages 4.0 pounds (1.8 kg). Body color is rusty to gray-brown, turning white in the winter. Ears retain their black tip in winter.**

**Track:** Toes asymmetrical around foot axis. Track indistinct because the foot is completely haired and lacks pads. Hind footprint may be up to two and a half times longer than front. To provide flotation on snow, hind feet are exceptionally wide and toes may splay apart so that width approaches length.

**Trail:** Hopping stride varies from 3.0 to 6.0 feet (0.9 to 1.8 m). Tends to hop with paired hind feet.

**Scat:** Dry scat is a slightly flattened sphere. Produces a black, semiliquid scat that is usually reingested to utilize remaining nutrients.

**scat**
0.3 in
0.8 cm

**chewed branch and cone**

SCAT WIDTH

**Habitat:** High mountains with deep snows. Dense second-growth forest is preferred, but swamps are also used. Forages at forest edge and in small clearings.

**Similar species:** Differs from cottontail by its large, wide size.

**Other sign:** Look for woody plants, including conifers, that have had the tips of branches chewed off. During population highs, hares will strip tree bark and have been observed feeding on carcasses. The snowshoe's nest, a shallow depression known as a *form,* is found under conifer branches or logs.

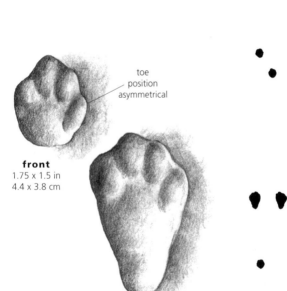

toe position asymmetrical

**front**
1.75 x 1.5 in
4.4 x 3.8 cm

**hind**
4.5 x 3.75 to 4.5 in
11.3 x 9.4 to 11.3 cm

**hop**

FRONT TRACK LENGTH

FRONT TRACK WIDTH

# American Pika
*Ochotona princeps*

Small (average 5.0 to 6.0 ounces/140.0 to 170.0 g), rat-size, short-legged, nearly tailless, egg-shaped member of the rabbit order (Lagomorpha). Large ears and relatively large eyes. Color gray to grayish brown. The pika of Alaska and the Yukon is the collared pika (*O. collaris*).

**Track:** Shows four toes. Only in a very clear footprint will the minute inside toe on the front foot be observed. Unlike the rest of the rabbit order, the pika's track shows toe pads. The sole is haired.

**Trail:** Prefers a hop, with a stride of 15.0 inches (38.0 cm). Even when moving fast, the stride is seldom more than three times the group.

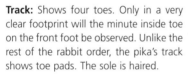

**scat**
0.1 in
0.3 cm

**hay pile**

**Scat:** Produces two types of scat. The most readily found are nearly spherical and dry. Also produces a black, semiliquid scat that is usually reingested to utilize remaining nutrients.

**Habitat:** Found almost exclusively in the rock and talus fields of high mountains.

**Similar species:** Differs from chipmunk and other rodents by having only four toes on hind foot. Track is larger than mouse or vole.

**Other sign:** Marks territory by urinating on prominent rocks, leaving a white, hard stain. Scat may be placed nearby. Stores plants under and around rocks near the center of its territory. These hay piles dry and provide food for the pika during winter.

**front**
0.75 x 0.6 in
1.9 x 1.5 cm

**hind**
1.0 x .075 in
2.5 x 1.9 cm

**hop**

FRONT TRACK LENGTH

FRONT TRACK WIDTH

# Mountain Beaver (Aplodontia)
*Aplodontia rufa*

Size of a large guinea pig, 2.0 to 3.0 pounds (0.9 to 1.4 kg). Dark brown and nearly tailless with small, rounded ears and small eyes. The aplodontia is a very primitive rodent that, although called a beaver, is only very distantly related to the true beaver, which is in another rodent family.

**Track:** Five toes with relatively long, wide claws on each foot. The inside toe of the front foot lacks a claw. Toes in the front print show a 1-4 grouping, toes in the hind a 1-3-1 grouping. The heel of the front foot is square, that of the hind footprint tapered.

**Trail:** Walking stride 6.0 to 8.0 inches (15.0 to 20.0 cm). Hind foot often understeps the front footprint.

**Scat:** Three to four times longer than wide and often tapered at both ends.

**scat**
up to 1.6 x 0.4 in
up to 4.0 x 1.0 cm

**open burrow with hay pile**

SCAT WIDTH

**Habitat:** Moist settings in dense forest. Favors loose soil and plant debris where it can build its burrow systems. Often present in logged areas.

**Similar species:** Distinguished from other rodents by front foot's inner toe lacking claw. Shape of the footprint is characteristic of this species only.

**Other sign:** Burrows are 4.0 to 8.0 inches (10.0 to 20.0 cm) in diameter and raised ground may show above ground. Burrows often cave in. After snow melt, solid casts of soil and rocks show where aplodontia packed dirt into tunnels in the snow while burrowing during winter. Aplodontia make hay piles to dry ferns and herbaceous plants for nest material and food storage. These are often on logs, not in rock fields, where those of pika can be found.

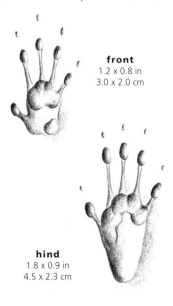

**front**
1.2 x 0.8 in
3.0 x 2.0 cm

**hind**
1.8 x 0.9 in
4.5 x 2.3 cm

**slow walk**

*track illustration based on information presented by Olaus Murie*

*FRONT TRACK LENGTH*

*FRONT TRACK WIDTH*

# Yellow-bellied Marmot
*Marmota flaviventris*

**Size of a large, fat domestic cat, 5.0 to 15.0 pounds (2.0 to 7.0 kg). Male larger than female. Ears and head are short and broad. Tail about one-third body length. Color brown to yellowish brown on back, yellow on belly.**

**Track:** Front foot size of a silver dollar, with four toes in 1-2-1 grouping. Five toes on hind foot, 1-3-1 grouping. Toes relatively slender. Four joined interdigital and two proximal pads on front footprint, and four joined interdigital pads on hind foot. Heel is hairless.

**Trail:** Bounding stride varies from 24.0 inches (60.0 cm) to 50.0 inches (125.0 cm). A ground dweller, the marmot uses a half bound.

**Scat:** Wide variety of forms, from oval pellets to long cords, all of which may be tightly stuck together. Sometimes lacks defined shape, being dark and runny when deposited. Deposited in "latrines" or "post offices" on top of prominent rocks and along ledges.

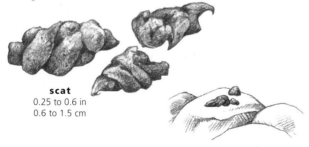

**scat**
0.25 to 0.6 in
0.6 to 1.5 cm

**scat on rocks**

**Habitat:** High mountain areas, especially those with talus and boulder fields. Larger boulders that protect tunnels against digging predators are preferred.

**Similar species:** Largest of the squirrels, its track dwarfs other ground squirrels. Track left when drinking at a stream may be distinguished from beaver's by lack of webbing and by having only four toes on front prints.

**Other sign:** May dig tunnels in nonrocky ground between boulder fields, probably as escape tunnels to be used when moving between rocky areas.

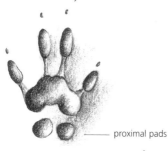

proximal pads

**front**
2.3 x 1.9 in
5.8 x 4.8 cm

**hind**
3.0 x 2.1 in
7.5 x 5.3 cm

**bound**

FRONT TRACK LENGTH

FRONT TRACK WIDTH

# Woodchuck
*Marmota monax*

**Size of a domestic cat, 5.0 to 10.0 pounds (2.2 to 4.5 kg). Ears and head are short and broad. Tail about one-third body length. Color frosted brown to yellowish brown on back but paler on belly, dark feet.**

**Track:** Front foot size of a silver dollar, with four toes in 1-2-1 grouping. Five toes on hind foot, 1-3-1 grouping. Toes relatively slender. Four joined interdigital and two proximal pads on front footprint, and four joined interdigital pads on hind foot. Heel is hairless.

**Trail:** Half bound stride varies from 15.0 to 40.0 inches (33.0 to 88.0 cm). A ground dweller, the woodchuck uses a half bound. Walking stride is 18.0 inches (40.0 cm).

**Scat:** Rare to find because it is deposited in latrines within tunnel systems. Wide variety of forms, from oval pellets to long cords, all of which may be tightly stuck together. Sometimes lacks defined shape, being dark and runny when deposited.

**scat**
0.25 to 0.5 in
0.6 to 1.3 cm

SCAT WIDTH

**Habitat:** Open or brushy areas, especially around rocky ravines and cultivated fields.

**Similar species:** Largest of the squirrels, its track dwarfs other ground squirrels. Track left when drinking at a stream may be distinguished from beaver's by lack of webbing and by having only four toes on front prints.

**Other sign:** Extensive tunnel system with two or more round-oval openings 5.0 to 7.0 inches (12.5 to 15.0 cm) in diameter. While some openings may have a large mound of dirt, others, excavated to the inside, may not have a mound and be more concealed. Fresh dirt indicates occupancy; if height of burrow exceeds 8.0 inches (18.0 cm), it may have been taken over by red fox.

proximal pad

**front**
2.2 x 1.8 in
5.5 x 4.5 cm

**hind**
2.8 x 2.0 in
7.0 x 5.0 cm

**bound**

*FRONT TRACK LENGTH*

*FRONT TRACK WIDTH*

# Hoary Marmot
*Marmota caligata*

Size of a large, fat
domestic cat, 10.0 to
20.0 pounds (4.5 to 9.0
kg). Male larger than female.
Ears and muzzle are short. Head
and shoulders are black and gray. Body is
yellowish gray. Feet are black. Brown hairy tail.

**Track:** Front foot larger than a silver dollar, with four toes in a 1-2-1 grouping. Five toes on hind foot, 1-3-1 grouping. Toes relatively slender. Four joined interdigital pads and two proximal pads on front footprint make the heel appear squarish. In the hind footprint, they give the heel a tapered appearance. Heel is hairless.

**Trail:** Bounding stride varies from 30.0 to 70.0 inches (75.0 to 175.0 cm). A ground dweller, the marmot uses a half bound.

**Scat:** Wide variety of forms, from oval pellets to long cords, all of which may be tightly stuck together. Sometimes lacks defined shape, being dark and runny when deposited. Deposited in "latrines" or "post offices" on top of prominent rocks and along ledges.

**scat**
0.25 to 0.7 in
0.6 to 1.8 cm

**scat on rocks**

**Habitat:** Found high in the mountains, near and above tree line. Uses talus slopes for den sites and refuge, but talus must be near grass meadows for feeding.

**Similar species:** Largest of the ground squirrels, its track dwarfs those of other squirrels. Track left when drinking at a stream may be distinguished from beaver's by lack of webbing and by having only four toes on front prints. Tracks distinguishable from the yellow-bellied marmot *(M. flaviventris)* of the eastern portions of the Pacific coast states and British Columbia only by their larger size, those of the hoary marmot's being 10 percent or more larger. Distinguished from raccoon by lack of an inner toe on the front foot.

**Other sign:** Burrow system with multiple openings, though dirt may be excavated through only one of the openings, allowing others to remain hidden.

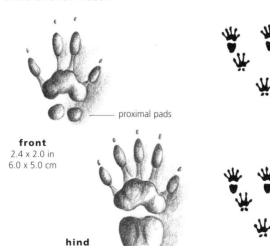

— proximal pads

**front**
2.4 x 2.0 in
6.0 x 5.0 cm

**hind**
0.25 x 0.6 in
0.6 x 1.5 cm

**bound**

FRONT TRACK LENGTH

FRONT TRACK WIDTH

# Blacktail Prairie Dog
*Cynomys ludovicianus*

Size of a large guinea pig,
2.0 to 3.0 pounds (1.0 to 1.4 kg).
Fat, yellowish brown ground
squirrel, with a black-tipped tail.
Lives in large colonies.

**Track:** Size of a quarter dollar. Long claws on front prints for digging. Four toes on front track, in 1-2-1 grouping (toe 5 does not show). Five toes on hind track, 1-3-1 grouping. Toes are relatively slender.

**Trail:** Bounding stride averages 30.0 inches (75.0 cm). Uses a half bound. Trots more than other squirrels.

**Scat:** Ranges from oval to a cord five to six times longer than it is wide. Scats are often connected by narrow filaments.

**scat**
0.1 to 0.2 in
0.3 to 0.5 cm

**mound and hole**

SCAT WIDTH

**Habitat:** Prairie and open grassland, where colony's "town" may consist of thousands of acres of low dirt mounds concealing tunnels.

**Similar species:** Differs from ground squirrel by the presence of longer digging claws. Claws longer and broader and feet smaller than those of tree squirrels. Smaller than marmot. Larger than mouse and vole.

**Other sign:** Colonies consisting of many burrows with elevated mounds and manicured "lawns" of grazed grass.

long claws

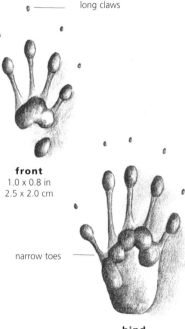

**front**
1.0 x 0.8 in
2.5 x 2.0 cm

narrow toes

**hind**
1.0 x 0.9 in
2.5 x 2.3 cm

**side lope**

**bound**

FRONT TRACK LENGTH

FRONT TRACK WIDTH

# Thirteen-lined Ground Squirrel
*Spermophilus tridecemlineatus*

**Size of a small rat, 0.25 to 0.5 pound (110.0 to 220.0 g). Body is light to dark brown, with 13 white stripes or rows of spots. White belly.**

**Track:** Front print has four toes, with 1-2-1 grouping. Hind has five toes, with 1-3-1 grouping. Toes relatively slender. Front footprint size of a quarter. Hind heel is hairless and may register clearly in track. Long claws may show, especially in front tracks.

**Trail:** Bounding stride averages 20.0 inches (50.0 cm). Uses a half bound, characteristic of its terrestrial lifestyle.

**Scat:** Small, usually unconnected ovals.

**burrow entrance**

**scat**
0.1 in
0.3 cm

SCAT WIDTH

**Habitat:** Found in grassy areas including pastures, cemetery lawns, golf courses, and along roadsides.

**Similar species:** Claws longer and feet smaller than those of tree squirrels. Smaller than woodchuck.

**Other sign:** Extensive burrow systems with a labyrinth of entranceways and galleries. Entrances are well hidden in vegetation and seldom have dirt at the entrances.

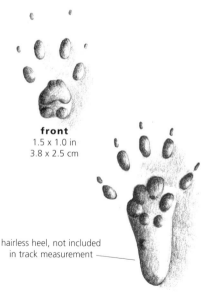

**front**
1.5 x 1.0 in
3.8 x 2.5 cm

hairless heel, not included in track measurement

**hind**
1.0 x 0.75 in
2.5 x 1.9 cm

**bound**

*FRONT TRACK LENGTH*

*FRONT TRACK WIDTH*

# Ground Squirrel
*Spermophilus* species

**Golden-mantled ground squirrel**
*S. lateralis*

Size of a small rat, 0.5 pound (225.0 g) and standing 8.0 inches (20.0 cm) tall. Golden-mantled ground squirrel *(Spermophilus lateralis)* has reddish gold shoulders and neck with white stripe bordered by black on sides of body (no stripes on face). Gray-brown on top of back. Haired tail. Uinta ground squirrel of the central Rocky Mountains *(Spermophilus armatus)* has light brownish fur spotted with white flecks. Fringe of white hair on edge of haired tail.

**Track:** Four toes with 1-2-1 spacing on front foot and five with 1-3-1 spacing on hind foot. Toes relatively slender. Front foot size of a quarter. Hind heel is hairless and may register clearly in track. Claws may show.

**Trail:** Bounding stride averages 15.0 inches (38.0 cm). Uses a half bound.

**Scat:** Small ovals, usually not connected.

**scat**
0.1 in
0.3 cm

SCAT WIDTH

**burrow entrance**

**Habitats:** Golden-mantled ground squirrel found in mountains with open pine or spruce-fir forest to upper tree line. Uinta ground squirrel found near edges of mountain meadows with open grass. Ranges in elevation to about 8,000 feet (2,400 m).

**Similar species:** *Spermophilus* species cannot be differentiated from one another by track. Habitat and visual identification necessary. Claws longer and feet smaller than those of tree squirrels. Lacks the long claws of prairie dogs. Smaller than marmot.

**Other sign:** The entrances to golden-mantled ground squirrel burrows are small and found under logs and rocks. Uinta ground squirrels live in colonies, which are indicated by many low mounds or moundless burrow entrances.

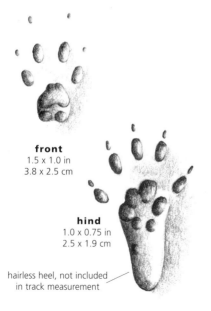

**front**
1.5 x 1.0 in
3.8 x 2.5 cm

**hind**
1.0 x 0.75 in
2.5 x 1.9 cm

hairless heel, not included
in track measurement

**bound**

*FRONT TRACK LENGTH*

*FRONT TRACK WIDTH*

# Franklin's Ground Squirrel
*Spermophilus franklinii*

**Size of a medium rat, 1.0 to 2.0 pounds (450.0 to 900.0 g). Body has brownish fur, graying on the head. Tail is long, bushy, and grayish brown in color.**

**Track:** Front print has four toes, with 1-2-1 grouping. Hind has five toes, with 1-3-1 grouping. Toes relatively slender. Front footprint size of a quarter. Hind heel is hairless and may register clearly in track. Long claws may show, especially in front tracks.

**Trail:** Bounding stride averages 25.0 inches (63.0 cm). Uses a half bound, characteristic of its terrestrial lifestyle.

**Scat:** Small, usually unconnected ovals.

SCAT WIDTH

**scat**
0.2 in
0.5 cm

**burrow entrance**

**Habitat:** A colonial squirrel found in low vegetation, including grasslands and open woodlands. Not found under dense timber.

**Similar species:** *Spermophilus* species cannot be differentiated from one another by tracks. Habitat and visual identification are necessary. Claws longer and feet smaller than those of tree squirrels. Lacks the long claws of prairie dogs. Smaller than marmots.

**Other sign:** Burrows have many openings. Runways, worn paths indicating repeated use, are found between burrow openings. Stores food in a den and makes a nest of dry vegetation.

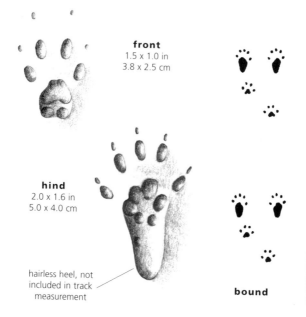

**front**
1.5 x 1.0 in
3.8 x 2.5 cm

**hind**
2.0 x 1.6 in
5.0 x 4.0 cm

hairless heel, not
included in track
measurement

**bound**

# California Ground Squirrel

*Spermophilus beecheyi*

Size of a small rat,
1.0 to 2.0 pounds
(450.0 to 900.0 g).
Body has brownish
fur spotted with white to
tan flecks. Back and top of
rump are darker in color.
Shoulders are tinted with white. Tail is bushy,
with white hair on the edge.

**Track:** Front print has four toes, with 1-2-1 grouping. Hind has five toes, with 1-3-1 grouping. Toes relatively slender. Front footprint size of a quarter. Hind heel is hairless and may register clearly in track. Long claws may show, especially in front tracks.

**Trail:** Bounding stride averages 25.0 inches (63.0 cm). Uses a half bound, characteristic of its terrestrial lifestyle.

**Scat:** Small, usually unconnected ovals.

**scat**
0.2 in
0.5 cm

SCAT WIDTH

**burrow entrance**

**Habitat:** Rocky areas with low vegetation in grasslands and open woodlands. Not found under dense timber or chaparral.

**Similar species:** *Spermophilus* species cannot be differentiated from one another by tracks. Habitat and visual identification are necessary. Claws longer and feet smaller than those of tree squirrels. Lacks the long claws of prairie dogs. Smaller than marmots.

**Other sign:** Burrows have many openings; underground portion is long, up to 200.0 feet (60.0 m). *Runways,* worn paths indicating repeated use, are found between burrow openings. Stores food in a den and makes a nest of dry vegetation.

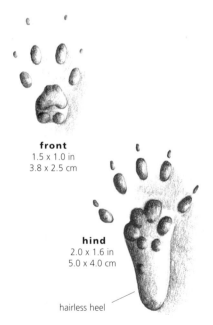

**front**
1.5 x 1.0 in
3.8 x 2.5 cm

**hind**
2.0 x 1.6 in
5.0 x 4.0 cm

hairless heel

**bound**

FRONT TRACK LENGTH

FRONT TRACK WIDTH

# Rock Squirrel
*Spermophilus variegatus*

Size of a large rat, about 1.5 pounds (700.0 g). Body is mottled gray mixed with red and brown. Head and back may be very dark. Long, bushy tail.

**Track:** Four toes with 1-2-1 grouping on front footprint and five toes with 1-3-1 spacing on hind. Toes relatively slender. Front footprint size of a quarter. Hind heel is hairless and may register clearly in track. Claws may show. More data is needed on track size.

**Trail:** Bounding stride averages 25.0 inches (65.0 cm). Uses a half bound, showing its terrestrial lifestyle.

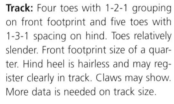

**scat**
0.2 in
0.5 cm

SCAT WIDTH

**burrow entrance**

**Scat:** Small ovals, usually not connected.

**Habitat:** Rocky areas with low vegetation in grasslands and open woodlands. Not found under dense timber or chaparral. Uses large boulders for lookout posts.

**Similar species:** *Spermophilus* species cannot be differentiated from one another by tracks. Habitat and visual identification necessary. Claws longer and feet smaller than those of tree squirrels. Lacks the long claws of prairie dogs. Smaller than marmot.

**Other sign:** Dens under large boulders. A loud, sharp whistle warns of danger and gives away its presence.

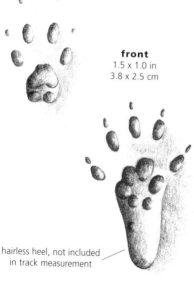

**front**
1.5 x 1.0 in
3.8 x 2.5 cm

hairless heel, not included
in track measurement

**hind**
2.0 x 1.6 in
5.0 x 4.0 cm

**bound**

FRONT TRACK LENGTH

FRONT TRACK WIDTH

# Arctic Ground Squirrel
*Spermophilus parryii*

Larger than a small rat,
1.0 to 1.5 pounds
(450.0 to 700.0 kg)
and standing
12.0 inches
(30.0 cm) tall. Males larger,
and both sexes put on weight as hibernation nears. White
spots on a reddish-brown back but turning grayish in fall.
Calls include a shrill whistle and chirp-chirp sound.

**Track:** Four toes with 1-2-1 spacing on front foot and five with 1-3-1 spacing on hind foot. Toes relatively slender. Front foot larger than a quarter. Hind heel is hairless and may register clearly in track. Claws may show.

**Trail:** Bounding stride about 20.0 inches (50.0 cm). Uses a half bound.

**scat**
0.1 in
0.3 cm

**burrow
entrance**

SCAT WIDTH

**Scat:** Small ovals, usually not connected.

**Habitat:** Found in higher mountain meadows and tundra above tree line. Often dens in ridges around polygonal or patterned ground.

**Similar species:** Only ground squirrel of this northern region.

**Other sign:** Look for burrow entrances.

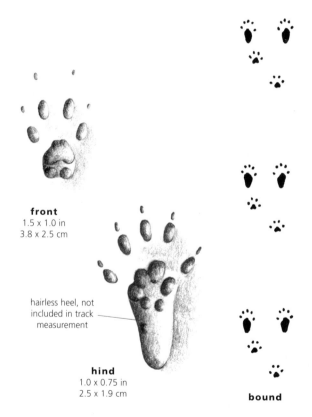

**front**
1.5 x 1.0 in
3.8 x 2.5 cm

hairless heel, not
included in track
measurement

**hind**
1.0 x 0.75 in
2.5 x 1.9 cm

**bound**

FRONT TRACK LENGTH

FRONT TRACK WIDTH

# Least Chipmunk
*Tamias minimus*

**Slightly larger than a large mouse, up to 3.0 ounces (80.0 g). Reddish fur, with white stripes bordered by black stripes along the sides of the face and body. Haired tail.**

**Track:** Front foot size of a nickel, with four toes in 1-2-1 grouping. Five toes on hind foot, 1-3-1 grouping. Toes relatively slender. Claws short. Hind heel is haired and details are difficult to detect.

**Trail:** Bounding stride averages 7.0 inches (18.0 cm). Mostly terrestrial, it usually uses a half bound, though full bounds may be observed in its trails.

**Scat:** Small, usually unconnected ovals.

**scat**
0.1 in diameter
0.3 cm

**Habitat:** Deciduous forest and brush areas.

**Similar species:** Smaller than ground and tree squirrels. Lacks the long claws of ground squirrel. Smaller than woodchuck. Tracks of chipmunk (*Tamias*) species are indistinguishable from one another.

**Other sign:** Seeds and nuts of various plants, chewed open on one side.

**front**
0.5 x 0.4 in
1.3 x 1.0 cm

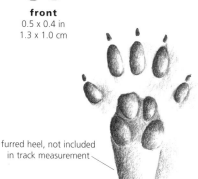

furred heel, not included in track measurement

**hind**
0.7 x 0.6 in
1.8 x 1.5 cm

**bound**

FRONT TRACK LENGTH

FRONT TRACK WIDTH

# Colorado Chipmunk
*Tamias quadrivittatus*

**Slightly larger than a large mouse, up to 3.0 ounces (85.0 g). Reddish fur, with white stripes bordered by black stripes along the sides of the face and body. Haired tail.**

**Track:** Nickel-size front foot, with four toes in a 1-2-1 grouping. Five toes on hind foot, 1-3-1 grouping. Toes relatively slender. Claws short. Hind heel is haired and details in the track are difficult to detect.

**Trail:** Bounding stride averages 7.0 inches (18.0 cm). Mostly terrestrial, it usually uses a half bound, though full bounds may be observed.

**Scat:** Small, usually unconnected ovals.

**scat**
0.1 in diameter
0.3 cm

*SCAT WIDTH*

**Habitat:** Varies, including coniferous forest and shrubland. Usually found near rocks.

**Similar species:** Smaller than ground and tree squirrels. Lacks the long claws of the ground squirrels and prairie dog. Smaller than woodchuck. Tracks of chipmunk (*Tamias*) species are indistinguishable from one another.

**Other sign:** Seeds and nuts of various plants, chewed open on one side.

**front**
0.5 x 0.4 in
1.3 x 1 cm

furred heel, not included
in track measurement

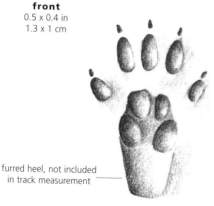

**hind**
0.7 x 0.6 in
1.8 x 1.5 cm

**half bound**

FRONT TRACK LENGTH

FRONT TRACK WIDTH

# Eastern Chipmunk
*Tamias striatus*

**Slightly larger than a large mouse, up to 3.0 ounces (80.0 g). Reddish fur, with white stripes bordered by black stripes along the sides of the face and body. Haired tail.**

**Track:** Front foot size of a nickel, with four toes in 1-2-1 grouping. Five toes on hind foot, 1-3-1 grouping. Toes relatively slender. Claws short. Hind heel is haired and details are difficult to detect.

**Trail:** Bounding stride averages 7.0 inches (18.0 cm). Mostly terrestrial, it usually uses a half bound, though full bounds may be observed in its trails.

**Scat:** Small, usually unconnected ovals.

**scat**
0.1 in diameter
0.3 cm

SCAT WIDTH

**Habitat:** Deciduous forest and brush areas.

**Similar species:** Smaller than ground and tree squirrels. Lacks the long claws of ground squirrel. Smaller than woodchuck. Tracks of chipmunk (*Tamias*) species are indistinguishable from one another.

**Other sign:** Seeds and nuts of various plants, chewed open on one side.

**front**
0.5 x 0.4 in
1.3 x 1.0 cm

furred heel, not included in track measurement

**hind**
0.7 x 0.6 in
1.8 x 1.5 cm

**bound**

*FRONT TRACK LENGTH*

*FRONT TRACK WIDTH*

# Eastern Gray Squirrel
*Sciurus carolinensis*

**Large squirrel, up to 1.5 pounds (0.7 kg). Grayish black with some brown in summer. Belly is whitish. Light-colored ring around eye. Tail is bushy, bordered with white hairs.**

**Track:** Front foot size of a half dollar, with four toes in 1-2-1 grouping. Five toes on hind foot, 1-3-1 grouping. Toes relatively slender. Claws relatively short. Haired hind heel is indistinct in tracks.

**Trail:** Bounding stride ranges from 24.0 to 36.0 inches (60.0 to 90.0 cm). Straddle 5.0 inches (12.5 cm). Tends to use a full bound.

**Scat:** Small, shapeless black masses to small, usually unconnected ovals.

**scat**
0.25 in
0.6 cm

**Habitat:** Hardwood forests and river bottoms. Nut-producing trees in territory.

**Similar species:** Larger than chipmunk. Lacks the long claws of ground squirrel. Larger than red squirrel and smaller than woodchuck.

**Other sign:** Nests in tree holes and builds twig-and-leaf nests in branches of trees, about 25.0 feet (7.6 m) from the ground.

hind
prints on
front

**slow bound**

**front**
1.6 x 1.0 in
4.0 x 2.5 cm

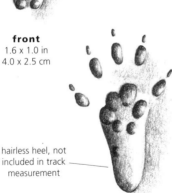

hairless heel, not
included in track
measurement

**hind**
2.6 x 1.4 in
6.5 x 3.5 cm

**full bound**

*FRONT TRACK LENGTH*

*FRONT TRACK WIDTH*

# Abert's or "Tassle-eared" Squirrel
*Sciurus aberti*

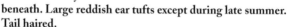

Large squirrel,
up to 2.0 pounds
(4.4 kg). Body
and tail color
variable. Back
reddish, sides
gray, belly white
or black. Tail may be
all white or only white
beneath. Large reddish ear tufts except during late summer.
Tail haired.

**Track:** Front foot size of a quarter, with four toes in a 1-2-1 grouping. Five toes on hind foot, 1-3-1 grouping. Toes relatively slender. Claws short. More data are needed on track size.

**Trail:** Bounding stride about 30.0 inches (75 cm).

**scat**
0.2 in
0.5 cm

**chewed cones
and seed casings**

SCAT WIDTH

**Scat:** Small, shapeless black masses to small, usually unconnected ovals.

**Habitat:** Restricted to ponderosa pine forests.

**Similar species:** Larger than chipmunk. Lacks the long, digging claws of ground squirrels. Differentiation from tree squirrels is only possible based on habitat.

**Other sign:** Uses large nests located high in pine trees. Its call may give its presence away.

hind prints
on front

**slow bound**

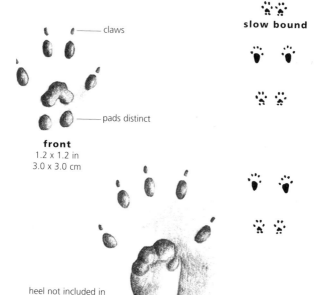

claws

pads distinct

**front**
1.2 x 1.2 in
3.0 x 3.0 cm

heel not included in
track measurement

**hind**
2.75 x 1.3 in
6.9 x 3.3 cm

**full bound**

FRONT TRACK LENGTH

FRONT TRACK WIDTH

# Pine or Red Squirrel
*Tamiasciurus hudsonicus*

Medium-size squirrel, up to 0.5 pound (225 g). Reddish-brown back, separated from white underparts by a black stripe. White ring around eye. Slight ear tufts. Tail is bushy.

**Track:** Front foot size of a quarter, with four toes in 1-2-1 grouping. Five toes on hind foot, 1-3-1 grouping. Toes relatively slender. Claws relatively short. Haired hind heel is indistinct in tracks.

**Trail:** Bounding stride averages 24.0 inches (60.0 cm). Tends to use a full bound.

**Scat:** Small, shapeless black masses to small, usually unconnected ovals.

**scat**
0.1 in
0.3 cm

**chewed cones
and seed casings**

SCAT WIDTH

**Habitat:** Boreal or northern coniferous forests. Infrequently found in deciduous forests.

**Similar species:** Larger than chipmunk. Lacks the long claws of prairie dog and ground squirrel. Smaller than marmot.

**Other sign:** Builds twig-and-leaf nests in branches of trees, about 15.0 feet (5.0 m) from the ground. Piles of pinecone scales (called *middens*) where squirrel removes scales to get at seeds. Cones are cached deep in the midden for use as winter food.

hind prints on front

**slow bound**

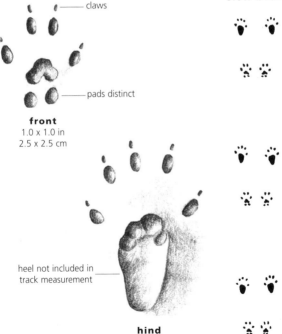

claws

pads distinct

**front**
1.0 x 1.0 in
2.5 x 2.5 cm

heel not included in track measurement

**hind**
0.9 x 1.0 in
2.3 x 2.5 cm

**full bound**

FRONT TRACK LENGTH

FRONT TRACK WIDTH

# Chickaree or Douglas' Squirrel
*Tamiasciurus douglasii*

Small to medium-size tree squirrel, less than 0.5 pound (226.0 g). Body is light gray with tints of red, especially on legs. Darker in winter. In summer, yellowish to orangish belly is separated from upper body by a black stripe on side.

**Track:** Front foot size of a quarter, with four toes in 1-2-1 grouping. Five toes on hind foot, 1-3-1 grouping. Toes relatively slender. Claws relatively short. Haired hind heel is indistinct in tracks.

**Trail:** Bounding stride averages 22.0 inches (56.0 cm). Tends to use a full bound, characteristic of its arboreal lifestyle. (Half bounds indicate a ground squirrel.)

**Scat:** Small, shapeless masses to small, usually unconnected ovals.

**Habitat:** Restricted to boreal or northern coniferous forests. Infrequently found in deciduous forests.

**scat**
0.1 in
0.3 cm

**chewed cones and seed casings**

SCAT WIDTH

**Similar species:** Larger than chipmunk. Lacks the long claws of prairie dog and ground squirrel. Smaller than marmot. Track slightly smaller than its more eastern relative, *T. hudsonicus,* which is found in Washington and Oregon.

**Other sign:** Builds twig and leaf nests in branches of trees. Also nests in hollow trees. Leaves piles of cone scales (called *middens*) where it removes scales to get at seeds. Cones are cached deep in the midden for use as winter food.

hind prints
on front

**slow bound**

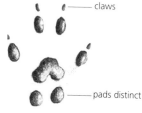

claws

pads distinct

**front**
0.9 x 0.8 in
2.3 x 2.0 cm

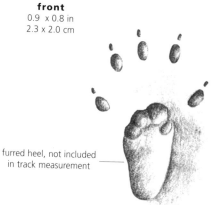

furred heel, not included
in track measurement

**hind**
0.8 x 0.9 in
2.0 x 2.3 cm

**full bound**

*FRONT TRACK LENGTH*

*FRONT TRACK WIDTH*

# Flying Squirrel—Northern and Southern

*Glaucomys sabrinus* and
*G. volans*

A small squirrel,
4.0 ounces (112.0 g).
Silky fur is olive brown
on the back and lead gray on the
underside. A fold of skin stretches
between front and hind legs and
body, forming a wing and
allowing the squirrel to glide.
Its bushy tail is flattened to aid in sailing.

**Track:** Front foot size of a quarter, with four toes in 1-2-1 grouping. Five toes on hind foot, 1-3-1 grouping. Toes relatively slender. Claws relatively short and may not show. Hind foot inter-digital pads form a tight crescent, though proximal pads are lacking.

**Trail:** Bounding stride averages 20.0 inches (50.0 cm). Uses a full bound.

**Scat:** Small, usually unconnected ovals.

**scat**
0.1 in
0.3 cm

**wing marks**

SCAT WIDTH

**Habitat:** Deciduous and coniferous forests, though often found in attics of houses.

**Similar species:** Differs from all other squirrels and chipmunks by the tight crescent of interdigital pads on the hind foot. Lacks the long claws of ground squirrels. Smaller than woodchuck.

**Other sign:** Skin flap outlines may show in dust or snow. Sometimes builds roof on bird nest to use as den. Tree dens may hold 20 squirrels during the winter.

hind prints
on front

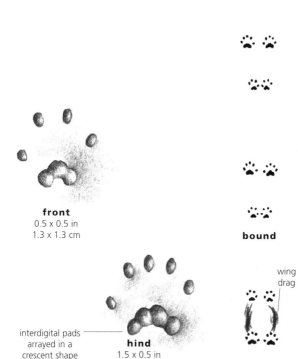

**front**
0.5 x 0.5 in
1.3 x 1.3 cm

**bound**

wing
drag

interdigital pads
arrayed in a
crescent shape

**hind**
1.5 x 0.5 in
3.8 x 1.3 cm

*FRONT TRACK LENGTH*

*FRONT TRACK WIDTH*

# Mice—Deer and White-footed
*Peromyscus* species

**Deer Mouse**
*Peromyscus maniculatus*

Small mice, up to 1.0 ounce (28.0 g). Adults are reddish brown to brown on back with a white belly, while juveniles are dark gray on the back with a light gray belly. Large eyes and ears. Tail is long and haired. There are many species of *Peromyscus*, but *P. maniculatus* (deer), illustrated here, and *P. leucopus* (white-footed) are most common across their range.

**Track:** Track smaller than a dime. Four toes on front foot, in 1-2-1 grouping. Five toes on hind foot, 1-3-1 grouping. Four joined interdigital and two proximal pads on front footprint; five joined pads and heel on hind footprint. Heel is hairless.

**Trail:** Bounding stride averages 8.0 inches (20.0 cm). Those species that use a full bound are climbers and nest in grass, shrubs, or trees. Those species using a half bound nest on or below ground. Both types occasionally trot. Tail drag may be present.

**scat**
0.1 in
0.3 cm

SCAT WIDTH

**Scat:** Oval-shaped pellets similar to those left by house mice.

**Habitat:** Ubiquitous, being found from deserts to the northern tree line, from below sea level to the top of high peaks.

**Similar species:** Differs from shrew by having only four toes on the front feet and by being slightly larger. Differs from vole by often showing a tail drag and by most often bounding. Lacks the long heel of the jumping mouse. Smaller than chipmunk.

**Other sign:** Compact grass nests without entrances may be found under logs, rocks, and boards. Enters and exits through the grass wall, which closes up after passage. Caches large quantities of seeds in any convenient protected area. Leaves feces near and in nest.

**tail drag**

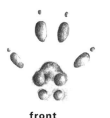

**front**
0.3 x 0.3 in
0.8 x 0.8 cm

**4 x 4 bound**

**hind**
0.4 x 0.3 in
1.0 x 0.8 cm

**3 x 3 bound**

*FRONT TRACK LENGTH*

*FRONT TRACK WIDTH*

# Bushy-tailed Woodrat
*Neotoma cinerea*

Rat-size, with a bushy, squirrel-like tail. Averages 1.0 pound (0.5 kg). Dusty brown on back, with gray face and whitish belly. Large eyes and ears. Also known as the pack rat of Western fables.

**Track:** Four toes on front foot, in 1-2-1 grouping. Five toes on hind foot, 1-3-1 grouping. Toes relatively slender. Toe pads are slightly constricted. Three joined interdigital, one remnant, and two proximal pads on front footprint and four joined pads and two proximal pads on hind. Feet have considerable hair, sometimes making prints appear large and indistinct.

**Trail:** Bounding stride 10.0 inches (25.0 cm). Walking stride 6.0 inches (15.0 cm). Bound is probably the most common gait, but walk is also common.

**Scat:** Small oval pellets.

**Habitat:** Prefers rocky areas, but will use houses and other human structures when available.

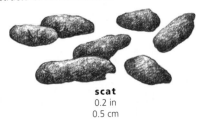

**scat**
0.2 in
0.5 cm

SCAT WIDTH

**Similar species:** Larger than mouse and vole. Differs from squirrels by the presence of heel pads on hind foot and by having constricted toe pads.

**Other sign:** Piles of sticks, cactus, bones, porcupine quills, and other debris tightly wedged in cracks in the rocks identify the pack rat home. Yes, this is where to look for missing keys, rings, glasses, and false teeth.

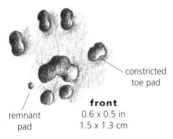

constricted toe pad

**front**
0.6 x 0.5 in
1.5 x 1.3 cm

remnant pad

**bound**

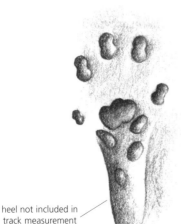

heel not included in track measurement

**hind**
1.5 x 0.9 in
3.8 x 2.3 cm

**fast walk**

FRONT TRACK LENGTH

FRONT TRACK WIDTH

# White-throated Woodrat
*Neotoma albigula*

**Size of a large house rat, 5.0 to 10.0 ounces (140.0 to 280.0 g). Hairless long tail is white below and brown above. Back gray to reddish, belly and throat white to light gray.**

**Track:** Four toes with 1-2-1 spacing on front foot and five with a 1-3-1 on hind foot. Toes relatively slender, and toe pads slightly constricted. Three joined interdigital, one remnant, and two proximal pads in front footprint and four interdigital pads and two proximal pads on hind print. Feet hairy, sometimes making prints appear indistinct and large.

**Trail:** Bounding stride is 14.0 inches (36.0 cm) and walking stride is 6.0 inches (15.0 cm). Bounding is probably the most common gait, but woodrats also commonly walk.

**Scat:** Small oval pellets.

**Habitat:** Arid grasslands and shrub country, usually with cactus.

**scat**
0.2 in
0.4 cm

**nest**

SCAT WIDTH

**Similar species:** Larger than mice and voles. Differs from squirrels by the presence of heel pads on hind foot. Tracks of woodrat (*Neotoma*) species are indistinguishable from one another.

**Other sign:** Constructs aboveground nests around the base of cactus using cactus spines and joints.

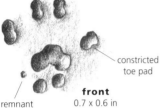

constricted toe pad

**front**
0.7 x 0.6 in
1.8 x 1.5 cm

remnant pad

**bound**

heel not included in track measurement

**hind**
0.9 x 1.5 in
2.3 x 1.6 cm

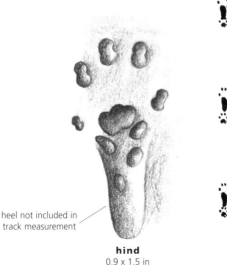

**fast walk**

# Mexican Woodrat
*Neotoma mexicana*

**Size of a small domestic rat, 0.3 to 0.5 pound (150.0 to 225.0 g). Body is gray, belly white, tail white below and blackish above. Relatively large ears. Hairless tail.**

**Track:** Four toes with 1-2-1 spacing on front foot and five with a 1-3-1 on hind foot. Toes are relatively slender and toe pads slightly constricted. Three joined interdigital, one remnant, and two proximal pads in front footprint and four interdigital pads and two proximal pads in hind footprint. Feet have considerable hair, sometimes making prints appear indistinct and large.

**Trail:** Bounding stride is 10.0 inches (25.0 cm), and walking stride is 6.0 inches (15.0 cm). Bounding is probably the most common gait, but woodrats also commonly walk.

**Scat:** Small oval pellets.

**nest**

**scat**
0.2 in
0.4 cm

SCAT WIDTH

**Habitat:** Prefers woodlands with rocky sites or cliffs. Also more in montane areas with mixed coniferous forests. Presence of rocks may be key.

**Similar species:** Larger than mice and voles. Differs from squirrels by the presence of heel pads on hind foot. Tracks of woodrat (*Neotoma*) species are indistinguishable from one another.

**Other sign:** Constructs nests of sticks, cactus, bone, porcupine quills, and other debris in cracks in the rocks and below ground. Large amounts of deposited and dried feces, called a *midden,* signal their presence. Middens may be 100,000 years old.

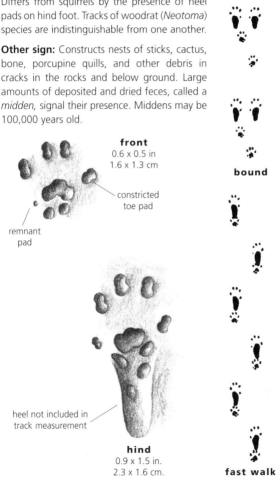

**front**
0.6 x 0.5 in
1.6 x 1.3 cm

constricted toe pad

remnant pad

heel not included in track measurement

**hind**
0.9 x 1.5 in.
2.3 x 1.6 cm.

**bound**

**fast walk**

FRONT TRACK LENGTH

FRONT TRACK WIDTH

# Eastern and Allegheny Woodrats
*Neotoma* species

**Eastern Woodrat**
*Neotoma floridana*

Size of a house rat, 10.0 to 16.0 ounces (280.0 to 450.0 g). Head gray, sides light brown; feet and belly are white. Densely haired long tail is white below and dark gray above. Back gray to reddish, belly and throat white to light gray. Large naked ears and long whiskers on face. Two similar species in the region are *N. floridana* (eastern) and *N. magister* (Allegheny). Tracks are difficult to distinguish.

**Track:** Four toes with 1-2-1 spacing on front foot and five with a 1-3-1 on hind foot. Toes relatively slender, and toe pads slightly constricted. Three joined interdigital, one remnant, and two proximal pads in front footprint and three interdigital pads and two proximal pads on hind print.

**Trail:** Bounding stride is 16.0 inches (40.0 cm) and walking stride is 6.0 inches (15.0 cm). Bounding is probably the most common gait, but woodrats also frequently walk.

**Scat:** Small oval pellets.

**nest**

**scat**
0.2 in
0.5 cm

SCAT WIDTH

**Habitat:** Limestone caves, cliffs, talus slopes and residual sandstone boulders in beech, poplar, and maple forest. Uses abandoned buildings, especially outhouses.

**Similar species:** Larger than mice and voles. Differs from squirrels by the presence of heel pads on hind foot.

**Other sign:** Bulky houses may contain two or more nests. Houses are made from dry grass, shredded bark, fur, feathers, and twigs. Caches of food, including nuts, berries, foliage, and mushrooms, may be found on nest. Nearby "post office" latrines on rocks may be used by several individuals, creating 2.0-inch (5.0-cm) deep masses of scat.

**bound**

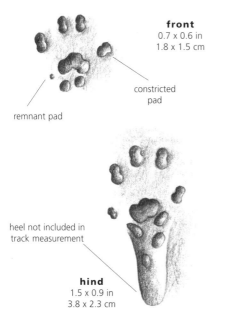

**front**
0.7 x 0.6 in
1.8 x 1.5 cm

constricted pad

remnant pad

heel not included in track measurement

**hind**
1.5 x 0.9 in
3.8 x 2.3 cm

**fast walk**

FRONT TRACK LENGTH

FRONT TRACK WIDTH

# Long-tailed Vole
*Microtus longicaudus*

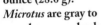

Mouse-size mammal related to the lemming and weighing up to 1.0 ounce (28.0 g). *Microtus* are gray to gray-brown on back, with a light colored belly. Stocky small mammals with short ears and small eyes almost hidden by their fur. Most voles have sparsely haired, short tails but that of the long-tailed vole is over 2.0 inches (5.0 cm).

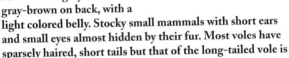

**Track:** Diminutive tracks smaller than a dime. Four toes on front foot, in 1-2-1 grouping. Five on hind foot, 1-3-1 grouping. Four joined interdigital and two proximal pads on front footprint and four interdigital pads and one proximal on hind footprint. Heel is hairless.

**Trail:** Trotting stride is 6.0 inches (15.0 cm). Usually trots and seldom bounds. Tail usually does not show in the trail.

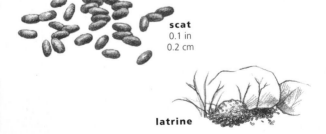

**scat**
0.1 in
0.2 cm

**latrine**

SCAT WIDTH

**Scat:** Typical mouse-shape ovals. Often placed in tennis ball–sized latrines consisting of thousands of pellets.

**Habitat:** Grass-loving species found near meadows and water holes in dry country.

**Similar species:** Differs from shrews by having only four toes on the front feet. Differs from mice by seldom showing a tail drag and usually trotting.

**Other sign:** In the spring as snow melts, look for grass nests lacking entrances but having cords of grass and debris. Cords were made when grass and debris were stuffed inside tunnels in the snow. Latrines are usually found near nests. Voles make worn runways through the grass.

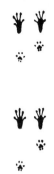

**bound**

**fast trot**

**front**
0.3 x 0.3 in
0.8 x 0.8 cm

**hind**
0.4 x 0.3 in
1.0 x 0.8 cm

five pads

heel not included in
track measurement

**trot**

FRONT TRACK LENGTH

FRONT TRACK WIDTH

# Meadow Vole
*Microtus pennsylvanicus*

One of many spe-
cies of mouse-size
mammals, related
to lemmings and up
to 3.0 ounces (80.0 g).
Gray to gray-brown on
back, with a light-colored
belly. Small, stocky mammal
with short ears and small eyes, almost hidden by fur. Short
tail is sparsely haired.

**Track:** Track smaller than a dime. Four toes on front foot, in 1-2-1 grouping. Five toes on hind foot, 1-3-1 grouping. Four joined interdigital and two proximal pads on front footprint and four interdigital pads and one proximal on hind footprint. Heel is hairless.

**Trail:** Trotting stride 6.0 inches (15.0 cm). Usually trots, seldom bounds. Tail usually does not show in the trail.

**Scat:** Oval-shaped pellets similar to those left by house mice, often piled in tennis ball–size latrines that may hold hundreds of pellets.

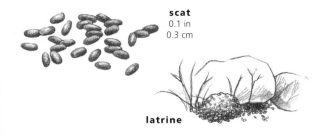

**scat**
0.1 in
0.3 cm

**latrine**

**Habitat:** Grass-loving species, found near meadows across North America and north to the Arctic.

**Similar species:** Differs from shrews by having only four toes on the front feet. Differs from mice by seldom showing a tail drag and by most often trotting. Lacks the long heel of the jumping mouse.

**Other sign:** As snow melts in spring, grass nests lacking entrances may be found. Snowmelt may also reveal 1.0-inch (2.5-cm) cords of grass and debris, stuffed into snow tunnels during winter to make space elsewhere in the tunnel network. Vole latrines are usually found near nests, while mice leave feces near and in their nests. Worn runways through the grass.

**bound**

**fast trot**

**trot**

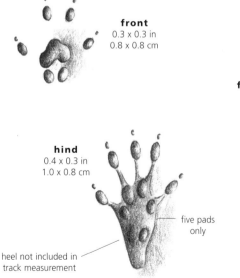

**front**
0.3 x 0.3 in
0.8 x 0.8 cm

**hind**
0.4 x 0.3 in
1.0 x 0.8 cm

five pads only

heel not included in track measurement

*FRONT TRACK LENGTH*

*FRONT TRACK WIDTH*

# Northern Collared Lemming
*Dicrostonyx groenlandicus*

**Large hamster-size rodent of the far north, up to 4.5 ounces (130.0 g). Another lemming, the brown lemming (*Lemmus trimucronatus*), also is found across northern regions. Lemming bodies** are stout with blunt noses, short tails, and small ears and tails. The collared lemming, dark gray in summer, turns white in winter and grows a digging claw.

**Track:** Track about the size of a dime, with hind footprint longer. Four toes on front foot, in 1-2-1 grouping. Five toes on hind foot, 1-3-1 grouping. Four joined interdigital and two proximal pads on front footprint and four interdigital pads and one proximal on hind footprint. More track and scat measurements are needed. We have only recorded blurred tracks in the snow.

**Trail:** Walking stride is up to 4.0 inches (10.0 cm). Straddle is 1.1 inches (2.8 cm). Brown lemmings usually walk or trot, collared lemmings often lope. Tails usually do not show in the trail.

**scat**
0.1 in
0.3 cm

**Scat:** Oval-shaped pellets similar to those left by house mice, often piled in tennis ball–size latrines that may hold hundreds of pellets.

**Habitat:** High dry areas with rocks and grass. Brown lemmings are found in tundra and alpine meadows.

**Similar species:** Differs from voles by having larger tracks and wider straddles on the trails. Differs from shrews by having only four toes on the front feet. Differs from mice by seldom showing a tail drag and by most often walking. Lacks the long heel of the jumping mouse.

**Other sign:** Piles of scat are common and usually mark winter latrines.

walk

**front**
0.4 x 0.4 in
1.0 x 1.0 cm

**hind**
about 0.6 x 0.4 in
about 1.5 x 1.0 cm

*FRONT TRACK LENGTH*

*FRONT TRACK WIDTH*

# Jumping Mice
*Zapus* species

Small—about 0.8 ounce (25.0 g)—mice with long hind feet and long, sparsely haired tail. Yellowish sides, darker brown back, and white belly. White tip on long tail. Common species in the west is *Z. princeps* (western); common species in the east is *Z. hudsonius* (meadow). Track and sign sizes are similar.

**Western Jumping Mouse**
*Zapus princeps*

**Track:** Four toes on front foot, in 1-2-1 grouping. Hind foot is about the size of a quarter, exceptionally long and narrow, and has five toes in 1-3-1 grouping. Toes relatively slender. Heel is hairless.

**Trail:** Bounding stride 60.0 to 120.0 inches (150.0 to 300.0 cm). Make sharp turns during travel. May cover considerable distance per stride when pursued. Tail drag often observed.

**scat**
0.08 in
0.2 cm

SCAT WIDTH

**Scat:** Small oval pellets.

**Habitat:** Mountains, seldom found more than 3.0 feet (1.0 m) from a stream.

**Similar species:** Differ from other rodents in having long, narrow hind feet and tail drag. Differ from kangaroo rat by bounding from all four feet, not just hind.

**Other sign:** Small piles of grass stems left after eating. Round grass nests.

tail drag

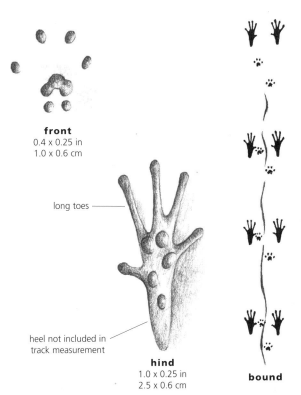

**front**
0.4 x 0.25 in
1.0 x 0.6 cm

long toes

heel not included in track measurement

**hind**
1.0 x 0.25 in
2.5 x 0.6 cm

**bound**

FRONT TRACK LENGTH

FRONT TRACK WIDTH

# Northern Pocket Gopher
*Thomomys talpoides*

Guinea pig–size
rodent with
minute eyes and
ears and a short
tail. Has external,
fur-lined cheek
pouches. Averages 12.0 ounces (340.0 g), with males larger
than females. Yellowish brown to dark, almost black. Two
distinct grooves down front teeth.

**Track:** Five toes front and hind foot. Toes are relatively slender. Front feet have relatively long, wide claws for digging. Claw length is equal to or longer than toe length. Good tracks are seldom found and more data are needed on track size. Measurements are approximate.

**Trail:** Walking stride is 6.0 inches (15.0 cm).

**Scat:** Thick, short cords.

**Habitat:** Needs deep sandy soils preferably associated with grass-lands, meadows, and fields.

**scat**
0.2 in
0.5 cm

**Similar species:** Differs from other rodents by large, wide claws.

**Other sign:** Summer mounds consist of loose dirt forming a flat mound with no entrance visible (gophers close the tunnel as they go back underground). Winter casts of soil and rocks show where gophers packed dirt into snow tunnels while they burrowed for food. Scat often found in the tunnel casts.

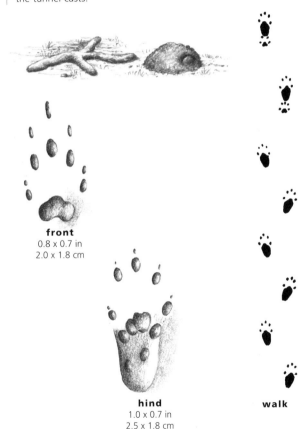

**front**
0.8 x 0.7 in
2.0 x 1.8 cm

**hind**
1.0 x 0.7 in
2.5 x 1.8 cm

**walk**

# Hispid Pocket Mouse
*Perognathus hispidus*

Large mouse, 1.0 to 1.7 ounce (28.0 to 48.0 g). Body color is mixed yellowish and brown. Hair is coarse. Tail shorter than head and body. Fur-lined, external check pouches. Largest of the pocket mice.

**Track:** Track about dime-size, though more data is needed. Four toes on front foot. Five toes on hind foot. The foot is hairy, and prints are often indistinct.

**Trail:** Bound stride is about 8.0 to 10.0 inches (20.0 to 25.0 cm). Uses a half bound.

**Scat:** Oval-shaped pellets similar to those left by house mice.

**Habitat:** Prefers sandy soils with short grass and other sparse vegetation.

**scat**
0.2 in
0.4 cm

**Similar species:** Differs from other mouse and vole species by indistinct track and occasional tail drag. Differs from shrews by having only four toes on front feet. Smaller than other rodent tracks.

**Other sign:** Burrows lack mounds. Stores caches of seeds often in depression on the ground surface.

**front**
about 0.4 x 0.4 in
1.0 x 1.0 cm

indistinct print

**hind**
0.5 x 0.4 in
1.3 x 1.0 cm

**hop**

FRONT TRACK LENGTH

FRONT TRACK WIDTH

# Plains Pocket Mouse
*Perognathus flavescens*

Small mouse, 0.3 to
0.6 ounce (8.0 to 16.0
g). Body color is
mixed yellowish and
brown. Hair is soft.
Tail as long as or lon-
ger than head and
body. Fur-lined,
external cheek pouches.

**Track:** Track about dime-size, though
more data is needed. Four toes on front
foot. Five toes on hind foot. The foot is
hairy and prints are often indistinct.

**Trail:** Bound stride is about 4.0 to 6.0
inches (10.0 to 55.0 cm). Uses a half
bound.

**Scat:** Oval-shaped pellets similar to
those left by house mice.

**Habitat:** Prefers sandy soils with short grass and other sparse
vegetation.

**scat**
0.1 in
0.3 cm

SCAT WIDTH

**Similar species:** Differs from other mouse and vole species by indistinct track and occasional tail drag. Differs from shrews by having only four toes on front feet. Smaller than other rodent tracks.

**Other signs:** Burrows lack mounds. Stores caches of seeds often in depression on the ground surface.

indistinct print

**front**
about 0.25 x 0.25 in
0.6 x 0.6 cm

**hind**
0.5 x 0.4 in
1.3 x 1.0 cm

**hop**

FRONT TRACK LENGTH

*FRONT TRACK WIDTH*

# Ord's Kangaroo Rat
*Dipodomys ordii*

Stocky and mouse-
size, about 2.0 ounces
(56.0 g), with large
hind feet and long,
fur-tipped tail.
Reddish brown on
back, white side stripe,
and dark belly.

**Track:** Feet have four toes. Long heel on hind foot may register. Feet are furred and toes difficult to distinguish.

**Trail:** Bounding stride averages 7.0 inches (18.0 cm) and typically ranges from 8.0 to 16.0 inches (20.0 to 40.0 cm). Often bounds on hind feet only. Tail drag often observed.

**Scat:** Small, usually unconnected ovals.

**Habitat:** Low-elevation animal. Prefers sandy soil where it can easily dig burrows.

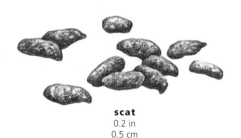

**scat**
0.2 in
0.5 cm

SCAT WIDTH

**Similar species:** Differs from western jumping mouse by greater width and more hair. May bound on the hind feet only.

**Other sign:** Scrapes out shallow "bathtubs" in dust as it dusts itself for protection against fleas.

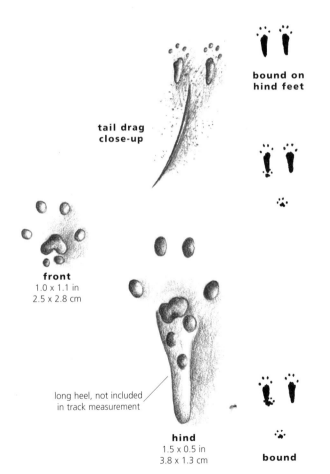

**bound on hind feet**

**tail drag close-up**

**front**
1.0 x 1.1 in
2.5 x 2.8 cm

long heel, not included in track measurement

**hind**
1.5 x 0.5 in
3.8 x 1.3 cm

**bound**

FRONT TRACK LENGTH

FRONT TRACK WIDTH

# Bannertail Kangaroo Rat
*Dipodomys spectabilis*

Size of a medium-size house rat, 4.0 to 10.0 ounces (110.0 to 250.0 g). A spectacularly colored rat with a prominent long tail (8.0 inches/20.0 cm). Body brownish, peppered with black hairs. White stripe along side. Tail is black with narrow white side stripes and a white tip.

**Track:** Hind foot has four toes (some species have five toes). Long heel on hind foot may register. Feet are furred, and toes may be difficult to distinguish.

**Trail:** Bounding stride about 20.0 inches (50.0 cm). Often bounds on hind feet only. Tail drag often observed.

**Scat:** Small, usually unconnected ovals.

**Habitat:** Open, dry grasslands with brush and shrubs, including mesquite and junipers.

**scat**
0.3 in
0.8 cm

SCAT WIDTH

**Similar species:** Differs from other kangaroo rats by the large size of the tracks. Differs from other mice by bounding on hind feet only—no front prints. Differs from most rodents by having only four toes in the hind track.

**Other sign:** Makes 10.0-foot diameter mounds from vegetation, debris, and dirt. Many openings lead to the den and seed caches. When people walk on the mounds, they often break through into the tunnels.

**bound on hind feet**

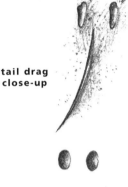

**tail drag close-up**

**front**
1.3 x 1.3 in
3.3 x 3.3 cm

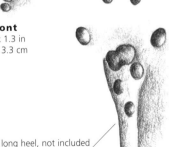

long heel, not included in track measurement

**hind**
about 2.0 x 1.0 in
5.0 x 2.5 cm

**bound**

# Nutria
*Myocastor coypus*

**Muskratlike
rodent 15.0 to
20.0 pounds (6.8
to 9.0 kg). Gray
to brown with
long, nearly
naked round tail.
Brought from
South America for fur farming and introduced into most of
the midwestern states. Thought to be eradicated. If you document their presence, contact wildlife officials.**

**Track:** Four toes on front foot (small toe
5 nubbin may show in very clear tracks)
and five on hind foot. Front print with
three interdigital and two proximal
pads. Hind print with five interdigital
pads and joined proximal pads. Hind
foot webbed except between toes 4
and 5. Detached claws.

**Trail:** Walking stride 12.0 to 14.0 inches
(30.0 to 35.0 cm). Occasionally gallops with one measured stride of
18.0 inches (45.0 cm). Walking straddle is 4.0 to 7.0 inches (10.0
to 18.0 cm).

**Scat:** We have not recorded their scat.

**Habitat:** Wetlands including marshes, swamps, and lakes.

**Similar species:** Four toes on front print and five toes on hind print identify as a rodent. Large size and webbing separate it from most other rodents. Lack of webbing between toes 4 and 5 separates it from beaver.

**Other sign:** Burrows in banks with entrances above water. Nest built in shallow-water vegetation.

**amble**

**front**
2.1 x 1.6 in
5.3 x 4.0 cm

**walk**

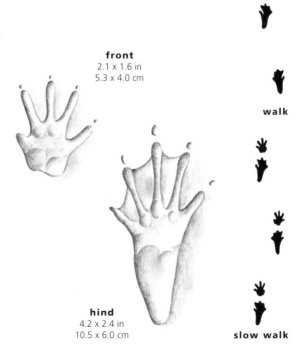

**hind**
4.2 x 2.4 in
10.5 x 6.0 cm

**slow walk**

*FRONT TRACK LENGTH*

*FRONT TRACK WIDTH*

# Beaver
*Castor canadensis*

**Largest rodent in North America, 30.0 to 60.0 pounds (14.0 to 27.0 kg). Distinguished by large, webbed hind feet and large, horizontally flattened tail. Fur overall is dark brown to almost black, with lighter belly.**

**Track:** Front and hind prints show five toes. Hind foot may be larger than a human hand. Webbing between hind toes shows, but only when pulled tight by splaying of toes. Clear tracks are difficult to find, as the hind foot steps on the front foot and the dragging tail obliterates many prints.

**Trail:** Walking stride 18.0 inches (45.0 cm).

**Scat:** Seldom found, as they are usually deposited in water, where they disintegrate quickly. Marshmallow-size, a little longer than thick. Consist of wood chips.

**scat**
1.0 x 0.7 in
2.5 x 1.8 cm

wood chips

**Habitat:** Seldom found far from a creek, river, pond, or lake.

**Similar species:** Differs from other rodents by large size and webbing. Differs from river otter by long, slender toes and pointed heel, and by lacking a chevron-shaped pad.

**Other sign:** Dams and conical lodges, built of twigs and sticks. Standing, cutoff tree trunks end in a tapered cone. Debarked tree limbs in the water.

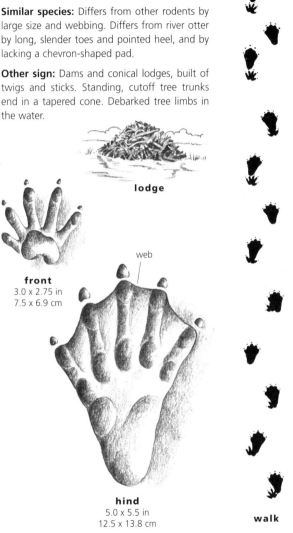

**lodge**

web

**front**
3.0 x 2.75 in
7.5 x 6.9 cm

**hind**
5.0 x 5.5 in
12.5 x 13.8 cm

**walk**

FRONT TRACK LENGTH

FRONT TRACK WIDTH

# Muskrat
*Ondatra zibethica*

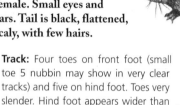

Large, ratlike, stocky, up
to 4.0 pounds (2.0 kg).
Male slightly larger than
female. Small eyes and
ears. Tail is black, flattened,
scaly, with few hairs.

**Track:** Four toes on front foot (small
toe 5 nubbin may show in very clear
tracks) and five on hind foot. Toes very
slender. Hind foot appears wider than
long.

**Trail:** Walking strides average 11.0
inches (28.0 cm). May lope with body
turned to side.

**Scat:** Oval, at most three to four times
longer than wide. Often deposited in a
sticky mass on exposed logs at water's edge.

**Habitat:** Marshes and lake edges, secondarily on streambanks.
Large rivers are not as frequently used. Cattails and rushes pre-
dominate.

**Similar species:** Differs from beaver by smaller size and lack of
webbing. Differs from mink by long, slender toes and by usually
walking.

**scat**
0.2 in
0.5 cm

SCAT WIDTH

**Other sign:** Small conical domes made from reeds serve as dens. Cut grass and reeds near water's edge mark feeding sites. Muskrats make "post offices," repeated scat deposits, on rocks.

**4 x 4 bound**

**3 x 3 bound**

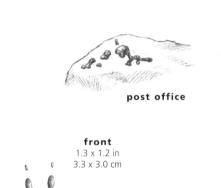

**post office**

**front**
1.3 x 1.2 in
3.3 x 3.0 cm

toe nubbin

— wide foot —

hair fringe

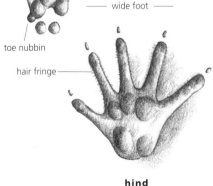

**side lope**

**fast walk**

**hind**
1.3 x 1.6 in
3.3 x 4.0 cm

**walk**

FRONT TRACK LENGTH

FRONT TRACK WIDTH

# Porcupine
*Erethizon dorsatum*

Basketball-size or larger, 10.0 to 25.0 pounds (5.0 to 11.0 kg). Stocky body, with short legs. Distinguished by the presence of quills. Brown to yellowish brown in color.

**Track:** Rough texture formed by small nubs on soles of feet. Four toes on front foot and five toes on hind. Toes often do not show. Claws often show.

**Trail:** Walking stride 17.0 inches (43.0 cm). Tail drag often present.

**Scat:** Winter scat formed from feeding on conifers is red. Summer scat includes more

**scat**
0.5 in
1.3 cm

**debarked stick with chew marks**

herbs and shrubs and is brown to black. Scat from both seasons may be composed of individual pellets or strings of pellets connected by fibers.

**Habitat:** Generally found near forests, but may be far from trees if shrubs are available.

**Similar species:** Rough texture on sole of foot is diagnostic. In snow, trough made by dragging belly highlights its stockiness, separating it from faster moving mammals.

**Other sign:** Twigs with bark chewed off, found at the bases of trees. Will perch in a tree for days, chewing the bark, thereby killing the tree.

tail drag

**amble**

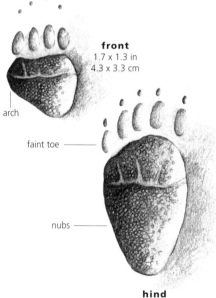

**front**
1.7 x 1.3 in
4.3 x 3.3 cm

arch

faint toe

nubs

**hind**
2.7 x 1.7 in
6.8 x 4.3 cm

**walk**

FRONT TRACK LENGTH

FRONT TRACK WIDTH

# Collared Peccary "Javelina"
*Dicotyles tajacu*

**Collie-size, up to 50.0 pounds (23.0 kg). North America's wild piglike mammal has mixed black and gray, coarse hair on the body. A white, often faint, collar rings the neck over the shoulders.**

**Track:** Silver dollar–size tracks with each clout rounded and blunt at the tip. Flat-bottomed hooves often do not leave much of a mark on the ground. Two dewclaws on front foot but only one on hind foot.

**Trail:** Walking stride is 23.0 inches (60.0 cm). The walking trail is often a set of rambling prints with many tracks registering close together as the javelina turns from side to side. Trotting stride is about 30.0 inches (80.0 cm). Its strange "rocking horse" gallop is a slow lope, but gallops may reach 100.0 inches (250.0 cm).

**Scat:** Consist of dry vegetation chips. Scat shape varies from oval to about three times longer than wide.

**scat**
1.2 x 1.6 in
3.0 x 1.4 cm

SCAT WIDTH

**Habitat:** Usually found near water holes or in dry streambeds. Prefers chaparral including oaks, mesquites, and cactus.

**Similar species:** Differs from deer by their blunt, rounded tips and rambling trails.

**Other sign:** The desert floor often shows disturbances caused while rooting for roots, nuts, fruits, insects, and eggs.

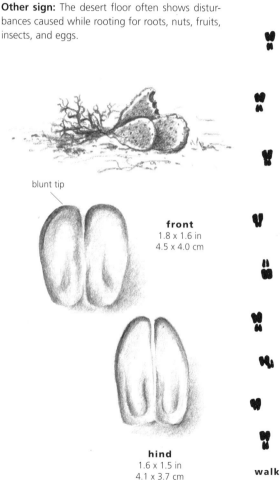

blunt tip

**front**
1.8 x 1.6 in
4.5 x 4.0 cm

**hind**
1.6 x 1.5 in
4.1 x 3.7 cm

**walk**

FRONT TRACK LENGTH

FRONT TRACK WIDTH

# Wild Boar / Feral Hog
*Sus* species

Medium-size to large pig, to more than 800.0 pounds (360.0 kg). Boars show great variability as they may be a mixture of European wild boars, recent domestic hogs, and 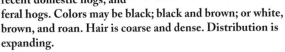 feral hogs. Colors may be black; black and brown; or white, brown, and roan. Hair is coarse and dense. Distribution is expanding.

**Track:** Deer-size tracks. Clouts are rounded and blunt at the tip. Hooves tend to splay. Dewclaws are more pointed and register up to 0.5 inch (1.3 cm) outside and up to 2.0 inches (5.0 cm) behind the hooves.

**Trail:** Walking stride is 25.0 inches (63.0 cm). Trotting stride is about 55.0 inches (140.0 cm).

soft

**scat**
pellet 0.4 in
pellet 1.0 cm

firm

SCAT WIDTH

**Scat:** Seasonally varies from formless on wet, spring diet to pellets to clumps of pellets on dry diets. Diameter of clumps of pellets may be over 2.0 inches (5.0 cm).

**Habitat:** Scattered distribution in swamps, marshes, and bottomland with mixed deciduous forests. Dense understory and moist soft soil is preferred. Raised dry areas for nests.

**Similar species:** Differs from deer by their blunt, rounded clouts, greater splay, and widely spaced dewclaws.

**Other sign:** Boars root up the earth and wallow. Trees are rubbed to 36.0 inches (90.0 cm). Nests are shallow depressions in dry ground occasionally lined with vegetation.

**walk**

**front**
2.5 x 2.1 in
6.3 x 5.3 cm

wide dewclaws

**trot**

**hind**
2.1 x 1.8 in
5.3 x 4.5 cm

*FRONT TRACK LENGTH*

*FRONT TRACK WIDTH*

# Bison
*Bison bison*

Large member of the cow family, with a large shoulder hump and massive skull. Male may weigh 1,500.0 pounds (680.0 kg), female about 1,300 pounds (590.0 kg). Head is dark brown to black, with the rest of the body brown. Calf is red overall. Both sexes have horns that are never shed. Horns of the male are larger.

**Track:** Very large, with round outer walls. Heavy bulls wear hooves down so much that the division between clouts may not be readily observable. Pad at back of clout forms a V.

**Trail:** Walking stride is 50.0 inches (125.0 cm). Usually walks, but occasionally lopes. When stampeding, uses a full gallop, and intergroup distances may reach 10.0 feet (3.0 m).

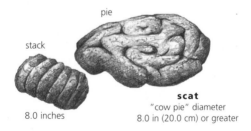

pie

stack

**scat**
"cow pie" diameter
8.0 in (20.0 cm) or greater

8.0 inches

**female horn**

**male horn**

SCAT WIDTH (50%)

**Scat:** Usually moist, forming "cow pies" much of the year. Young bison scat appears as a stack of cookie-size wafers.

**Habitat:** Grassland and open mountain meadows. Nowadays, herds are found only in national and state parks, and on private ranches in some areas.

**Similar species:** Differs from moose track by having rounded wall outline and rounded tips. Larger than other hoofed animals.

**Other sign:** The most conspicuous sign of the bison is its wallow, a large depression where both sexes roll around, usually in dry dirt, but occasionally in wet areas.

**lope**

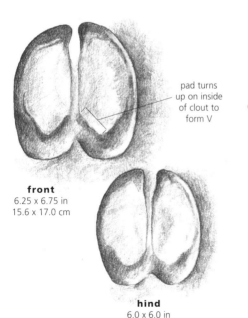

pad turns up on inside of clout to form V

**front**
6.25 x 6.75 in
15.6 x 17.0 cm

**hind**
6.0 x 6.0 in
15.0 x 15.0 cm

**walk**

# Moose
*Alces alces*

Largest member of deer family. Considerable regional variation exists, but male may weigh 900.0 pounds (400.0 kg), with female smaller. Color varies from tan to blackish. Females have a white patch of hair around the vulva (visible at a distance) that helps identify sex. Male has antlers that are shed annually.

**Track:** Long, with the pad extending to near the front of the hoof. Subunguinis region is narrow. Track is delicate for the weight of the animal.

**Trail:** Walking stride is 70.0 inches (175.0 cm). Seldom gallops. Trots when in a hurry.

**Scat:** Most of the year, consists of dry pellets that scatter on impact with the ground. When the diet is moist, nipple-dimple shape predominates. Winter scat is oval and consists mostly of chips of woody vegetation.

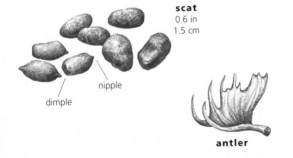

**scat**
0.6 in
1.5 cm

nipple

dimple

antler

**Habitat:** Mixed conifer and hardwood forests containing willows and quaking aspen. Streams and shallow lakes provide aquatic vegetation.

**Similar species:** Differs from elk in that the pad occupies most of each clout. Differs from deer by being larger and more pointed. Differs from bison by having long rather than round track.

**Other sign:** In removing velvet from their antlers, bulls strip bark from young saplings and break off limbs, often killing the trees. Height of tree wound shows animal height.

**trot**

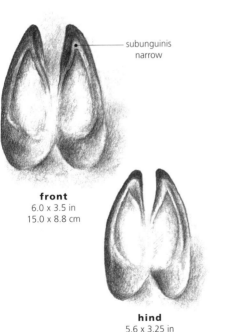

subunguinis narrow

**front**
6.0 x 3.5 in
15.0 x 8.8 cm

**hind**
5.6 x 3.25 in
14.0 x 8.2 cm

**walk**

FRONT TRACK LENGTH

FRONT TRACK WIDTH

# Caribou
*Rangifer tarandus*

Smaller than elk, larger than deer, with males averaging 250.0 pounds (115.0 kg) and females 225.0 pounds (100.0 kg). The tines (points) over the nose are palmate (webbed). Fur color is gray to grayish brown. Males and females have antlers that are shed annually. Those of males are larger.

**Track:** Track is wide or wider than long. Hoof walls rounded on the outside, making hoof appear almost circular. Dewclaw impressions are widely spaced.

**Trail:** Walking stride is 48.0 inches (120.0 cm). Trotting stride 75.0 inches (188.0 cm). Caribou walk when grazing, but when moving longer distances, they tend to trot, with hind foot overstepping the front.

**Scat:** Typical scat is dry, falling apart when it hits the ground.

**scat**
pellet 0.4 in
pellet 1.0 cm

**antler**

SCAT WIDTH

**Habitat:** The southern limit of range barely reaches the lower 48 states. Habitat includes mountain summits above tree line and alpine meadows interspersed with open subalpine forests.

**Similar species:** Differs from other hoofed animals by its round, wide print and widely spaced dewclaws. Rounded tips of hoof distinguish caribou prints from those of bison.

**Other sign:** Large herds leave wide travel route. Snow may be scraped from ground to get at lichens, which caribou eat.

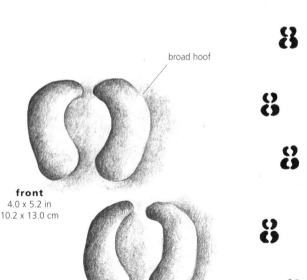

broad hoof

**front**
4.0 x 5.2 in
10.2 x 13.0 cm

**hind**
3.1 x 3.6 in
8.0 x 9.0 cm

**fast walk**

*FRONT TRACK LENGTH*

*FRONT TRACK WIDTH (50%)*

# White-tailed Deer
*Odocoileus virginianus*

Smallest member of the deer family. Male averages 130.0 pounds (60.0 kg), female 110.0 pounds (50.0 kg). Coat is reddish in summer and blue-gray in winter. The prominent white tail is carried erect when animal is disturbed. Antlers, found only on male, have tines, or points, branching off main beam.

**Track:** Heart-shaped, with convex wall. Pad occupies most of the clout; subunguinis slender.

**Trail:** Walking stride 30.0 inches (75.0 cm). Pronks or stots with front and hind feet striking the ground at the same time. Gallops when in a hurry.

**Scat:** Usually dry, falls apart when it hits the ground. Pellets vary from nipple-dimple shape to oval.

**scat**
pellet 0.3 in
pellet 0.8 cm

**antler**

SCAT WIDTH

**Habitat:** Generally closed timber, but moves out to grasslands at twilight to feed.

**Similar species:** Smaller than elk, has more slender tips, and pad occupies most of clout.

**Other sign:** Gathers (yards up) in large numbers in sheltered groves during the winter. Breaks off limbs of trees when removing the velvet from antlers. Velvet is difficult to find, as both deer and rodents eat the nutrient-rich material. Height of tree wound indicates animal height.

**pronk**

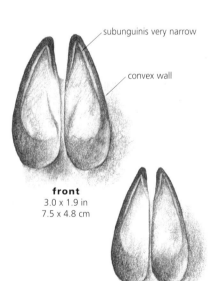

subunguinis very narrow

convex wall

**front**
3.0 x 1.9 in
7.5 x 4.8 cm

**hind**
2.6 x 1.5 in
6.5 x 3.8 cm

**gallop**

*FRONT TRACK LENGTH*

*FRONT TRACK WIDTH*

# Mule Deer
*Odocoileus hemionus*

Small member of the deer family, male averaging 160.0 pounds (70.0 kg) and female 130.0 pounds (60.0 kg). Coat color is reddish brown in summer and grayish brown in the winter. Antlers, found only on males, branch symmetrically and are shed annually.

**Track:** Heart-shaped, with convex wall. Pad occupies most of the clout; subunguinis slender.

**Trail:** Walking stride is 36.0 inches (90.0 cm). Pronks or stots with front and hind feet striking the ground at the same time. Gallops when in a hurry.

**Scat:** Usually dry, falls apart when lands on the ground. Pellets vary from nipple-dimple shape to oval.

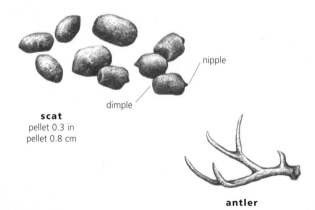

nipple

dimple

**scat**
pellet 0.3 in
pellet 0.8 cm

**antler**

SCAT WIDTH

**Habitat:** Foothills are prime habitat, where can frequent open brush interspersed with rugged terrain. Found in all vegetation zones except in the Arctic and in extreme desert.

**Similar species:** Track is not distinguishable from white-tailed deer, although mule deer is usually larger. Differs from pronghorn, goats, and sheep by having convex walls. Smaller than elk, has more slender tips, and pad occupies most of clout.

**Other sign:** Breaks off limbs of trees when removing the velvet from antlers. Velvet is difficult to find, as both deer and rodents eat the nutrient-rich material. Height of tree wound indicates height of animal.

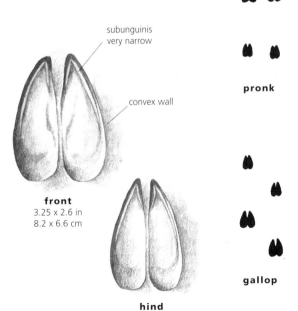

subunguinis
very narrow

convex wall

**front**
3.25 x 2.6 in
8.2 x 6.6 cm

**hind**
3.1 x 2.5 in
7.8 x 6.3 cm

**pronk**

**gallop**

FRONT TRACK LENGTH

FRONT TRACK WIDTH

# Elk
*Cervus elaphus*

**Medium-size, larger than deer, males averaging 700.0 pounds (315.0 kg) and females 450.0 pounds (200.0 kg). Reddish to dark brown, with a yellow rump patch. Males shed antlers annually. Also known as wapiti. Reintroduced in East.**

**Track:** Blocky, with each clout wide at the leading tip. Pad of hoof occupies rear third of each clout; subunguinis occupies remaining two-thirds of each clout.

**Trail:** Walking stride 52.0 inches (130.0 cm). When chased by a predator, gallops and occasionally pronks.

**Scat:** Most of the year, scat consists of pellets that scatter on impact with the ground. When the diet is moist, nipple-dimple shape predominates, changing to oval as vegetation dries. When scat is moist, pellets stick together.

nipple

dimple

**scat**
pellet 0.5 in
pellet 1.3 cm

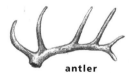

**antler**

*SCAT WIDTH*

**Habitat:** Forest. Beds in dense trees during the day, moving out into clearings to graze during twilight hours.

**Similar species:** Differs from deer and moose by having a small pad at the rear of the hoof.

**pronk**

**Other sign:** Removing antler velvet, bulls strip bark from young saplings and break off limbs, often killing the trees. Height of tree wound shows animal height. Bulls make mud wallows in the fall. During rut, look for areas where bulls have sparred with the ground using their antlers.

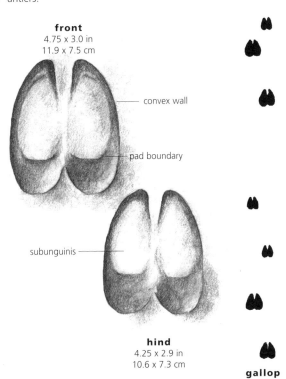

**front**
4.75 x 3.0 in
11.9 x 7.5 cm

convex wall

pad boundary

subunguinis

**hind**
4.25 x 2.9 in
10.6 x 7.3 cm

**gallop**

# Pronghorn Antelope
*Antilocapra americana*

Smaller than deer,
found only in North
America. Male averages
125.0 pounds (56.0 kg),
female 110.0 pounds
(50.0 kg). White and
tan to reddish brown,
with black and brown
markings on the head
and neck. Both sexes
have forked horns that
are shed annually.

**Track:** Identified by the concave outline of the wall, which bends slightly
inward at a point about one-third of
the way back from the tip. Pad is
bulbous. Lacks dewclaws.

**Trail:** Ambling stride 35.0 inches
(88.0 cm). Most common gait is an
*amble*, a fast walk where the hind
foot registers slightly in front of the front footprint. Often uses a

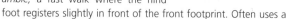

**scat**
pellet 0.3 in
pellet 0.8 cm

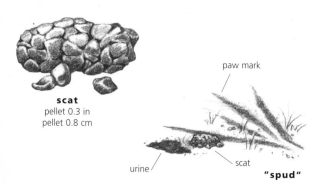

paw mark

urine

scat

**"spud"**

SCAT WIDTH

Z-shaped gallop, with a stride ranging from 80.0 to 145.0 inches (200.0 to 363.0 cm).

**Scat:** Typically, well-defined pellets that often stay together upon impact with the ground.

**Habitat:** Open and shrub country of short- to midgrass prairie. Herbs and winter browse above the snow are important. Commonly found with sagebrush.

**Similar species:** Differentiated from deer by its small size and concave wall. Lacks dewclaws.

**Other sign:** The territorial marking of the male pronghorn is a *spud,* produced as the male **s**niffs and **p**aws the ground after **u**rinating and **d**efecating to spread the odor.

**gallop**

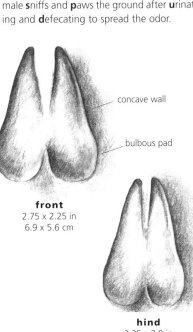

concave wall

bulbous pad

**front**
2.75 x 2.25 in
6.9 x 5.6 cm

**hind**
2.25 x 2.0 in
5.6 x 5.0 cm

**amble**

FRONT TRACK LENGTH

FRONT TRACK WIDTH

# Bighorn Sheep
*Ovis canadensis*

Medium-size sheep, distinguished by massive horns of the male. Male averages 300.0 pounds (135.0 kg), female 200.0 pounds (90.0 kg). Light brown, white rump and muzzle. Ram has spiraled horn; ewe's is small and straight. Horns are not forked and are never shed. Two subspecies of bighorn are recognized: Rocky Mountain (*Ovis c. canadensis*) and desert (*O. c. californiana*).

**Track:** Blocky, with edges of the walls straight along the sides.

**Trail:** Trotting stride 70.0 inches (175.0 cm). Most common gait is a walk with 36.0-inch (90.0-cm) stride, but trotting is common in open country.

**Scat:** More likely to be dry and to separate into pellets than that of other hoofed mammals.

**Habitat:** High mountain areas, especially along cliffs. Comes down from cliffs for water, and grazes on grass in rolling hills. Migrates below timberline during the winter.

**scat**
pellet 0.3 in
pellet 0.8 cm

SCAT WIDTH

**Similar species:** Wall differs from antelope and deer by having a straight edge. Shows dewclaws, which antelope does not. Differs from deer and elk by relatively large subunguinis region of the clout.

**Other sign:** Beds scraped in soil along the edges of cliffs; deposits of old scat at repeatedly used beds may be considerable. Mineral and salt licks often serve as a focus of activity.

male horn

female horn

wall straight along sides

**front**
3.5 x 2.5 in
8.8 x 6.3 cm

**hind**
3.0 x 2.0 in
7.5 x 5.0 cm

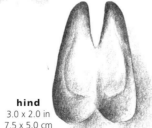

**trot**

*FRONT TRACK LENGTH*

*FRONT TRACK WIDTH*

# Thinhorn Sheep
*Ovis dalli*

**Dall sheep**
*Ovis dalli*

Medium-size sheep, distinguished by massive horns of the male. Male averages 180.0 pounds (80.0 kg), female about two-thirds the size of the male. Two subspecies exist: *O. d. dalli* is uniformly white and *O. d. stonei* is grayish brown with a white muzzle. Northern populations consist of white Dall sheep, and southern populations consist of Stone sheep. Stone sheep are slightly larger than Dall sheep. Ram has spiraled horn; ewe's is small and straight. Horns are not forked and are never shed.

**Track:** Blocky, with edges of the walls straight along the sides.

**Trail:** Walking stride is 35.0 inches (90.0 cm). Stride of a galloping Dall sheep, perhaps pursued by a wolf, was 106.0 inches (270.0 cm).

**scat**
0.3 in
0.8 cm

SCAT WIDTH

**Scat:** More likely to be dry and to separate into pellets than that of other hoofed mammals.

**Habitat:** High mountain areas, especially along cliffs. Comes down from cliffs for water, and grazes on grass in rolling hills. Migrates to lower range during the winter.

**Similar species:** Wall differs from pronghorn and deer by having a straight edge. Shows dewclaws, which pronghorn do not. Differs from deer and elk by relatively large subunguinis region of the clout.

**Other sign:** Beds scraped in soil along the edges of cliffs; deposits of old scat at repeatedly used beds may be considerable. Mineral and salt licks often serve as a focus of activity.

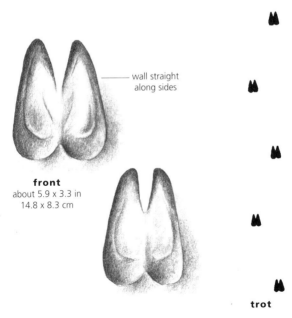

wall straight along sides

**front**
about 5.9 x 3.3 in
14.8 x 8.3 cm

**trot**

FRONT TRACK LENGTH

FRONT TRACK WIDTH

# Muskox
*Ovibos moschatus*

Large bisonlike mammal weighing 400.0 to 900.0 pounds (180.0 to 400.0 kg). Cashmerelike brown wool hangs nearly to the ground. Light gray saddle on shoulders. Few people ever see this creature of the north; my experience with them was in Greenland.

**Track:** Each half of the hoof is rounded, with the over impression being of a rounded footprint.

**Trail:** Walking stride is about 40.0 inches (100.0 cm).

**Scat:** Dry, large pellets and cowpielike in early summer.

**Habitat:** Grassy areas in summer but seeks out wind-clear spots in the winter.

**scat**
pellet 0.5 in
pellet 1.3 cm

SCAT WIDTH

**Similar species:** Hoof is more robust than that of the caribou.

**Other sign:** Main indicators of muskoxen are large deposits of scat and wallowlike beds.

**front**
about 5.5 x 5.0 in
13.8 x 12.5 cm

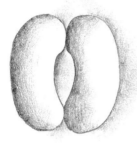

**hind**
about 4.5 x 4.0 in
11.3 x 10.0 cm

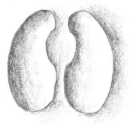

**walk**

*FRONT TRACK LENGTH*

*FRONT TRACK WIDTH (50%)*

# Mountain Goat
*Oreamnos americanus*

Sheep-size mammal,
found only in North
America. Male averages
300.0 pounds (135.0 kg),
female about 200.0 pounds
(90.0 kg). Predominantly white,
and distinguished by a stocky
build and hump on shoul-
ders. Horns, which are not
shed, are straight, about
10.0 inches (25.0 cm). Those of female slightly smaller.

**Track:** Footprint is blocky. Tip of the clout occurs in the middle of each clout, not to the inside as in other hoofed mammals. Relatively large subunguinus.

**Trail:** Walking stride is about 30.0 inches (75.0 cm). Goats most often walk.

**Scat:** Tends to be dry and separates when it hits the ground.

**scat**
pellet 0.4 in
pellet 1.0 cm

SCAT WIDTH

**horn**

**Habitat:** High mountains, on the steepest crags and cliffs. May bed among rocks, or in snow-banks or vegetated areas. Caves may be used as shelter from sun or wind. Windblown slopes are used for feeding in the winter.

**Similar species:** Differs from all other hoofed mammals by the location of tip in the middle of each clout.

**Other sign:** Digs dry wallows (shallow depressions) in the summer. Mineral or salt licks attract activity.

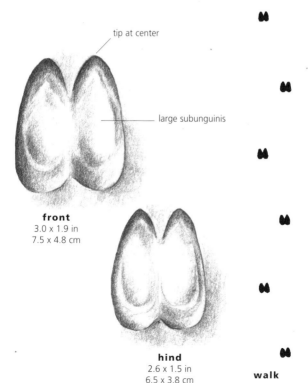

tip at center

large subunguinis

**front**
3.0 x 1.9 in
7.5 x 4.8 cm

**hind**
2.6 x 1.5 in
6.5 x 3.8 cm

**walk**

FRONT TRACK LENGTH

FRONT TRACK WIDTH

# Selected reading

## Tracks and tracking

Bang, P. et al. 1972. *Collins Guide to Animal Tracks and Signs.* London: Collins Sons.

Brown, R., J. Ferguson, M. Lawrence, and D. Lees. 1987. *Tracks and Signs of the Birds of Britain and Europe: An Identification Guide.* Kent, England: Christopher Helm.

Elbroch, M. 2003. *Mammal Tracks and Sign: A Guide to North American Species.* Mechanicsburg, PA: Stackpole Books.

—. 2001. *Bird Tracks and Sign: A Guide to North American Species.* Mechanicsburg, PA: Stackpole Books.

Fjelline, D. P., and T. M. Mansfield. 1989. Method to standardize the procedure for measuring mountain lion tracks. In *Proceedings of the Third Mountain Lion Workshop,* ed. R. H. Smith, 49–51. Prescott, AZ: Arizona Game and Fish Department.

Forrest, L. R. 1988. *Field Guide to Tracking Animals in Snow.* Harrisburg, PA: Stackpole Books.

Halfpenny, J. C. 1997. *Tracking: Mastering the Basics.* 180 min. A Naturalist's World. Videocassette and CD.

—. 1986a. *A Field Guide to Mammal Tracking in North America.* Boulder, CO: Johnson Books.

—. 1986b. *Tracks and Tracking: A "How to" Guide.* Gardiner, MT: A Naturalist's World. Slides.

Halfpenny, J. C. et al. 1996. Snow tracking. In *American Marten, Fisher, Lynx, and Wolverines: Survey Methods for Their Detection,* eds. W. Zielinski and T. Kucera, 91–163. General Technical Report PSW-GTR-157. Berkeley, CA: USDA Forest Service, Pacific Southwest Research Station.

Headstrom, R. 1971. *Identifying Animal Tracks: Mammals, Birds, and Other Animals of the Eastern United States.* New York: Dover.

Lowery, J. C. 2006. *The Tracker's Field Guide.* FalconGuide. Guilford, CT: The Globe Pequot Press.

Murie, O. and M. Elbroch. 2005. *A Field Guide to Animal Tracks.* 3rd ed. Peterson Field Guide Series, no. 9. Boston: Houghton Mifflin.

Rezendes, P. 1999. *Tracking and the Art of Seeing: How to Read Animal Tracks and Sign.* 2nd ed. Charlotte, VT: Camden House.

Seton, E. T. 1958. *Animal Tracks and Hunter Signs.* New York: Doubleday.

## Recommended field identification guides

Burt, W. H., and R. P. Grossenheider. 1964. *A Field Guide to the Mammals.* Peterson Field Guide Series no. 5. Boston: Houghton Mifflin.

Conant, R. 1958. *Reptiles and Amphibians of Eastern and Central North America.* Peterson Field Guide Series no. 12. Boston: Houghton Mifflin.

Kays, R. W., and D. E. Wilson. 2002. *Mammals of North America.* Princeton, NJ: Princeton University Press.

National Geographic Society. 1983. *Field Guide to the Birds of North America.* Washington, D.C.: National Geographic Society.

Peterson, R. T. 1984. *Birds of the Eastern United States.* Norwalk, CT: The Easton Press.

Sibley, D. A. 2003. *The Sibley Field Guide to Birds of Western North America.* New York: Alfred A. Knopf, Inc.

Sibley, D. A. 2000. National Audubon Society. *The Sibley Guide to Birds.* New York: Alfred A. Knopf, Inc.

Stebbins, R. C. 1985. *A Field Guide to Western Reptiles and Amphibians.* Peterson Field Guide Series, no. 16. Boston: Houghton Mifflin.

# Index

**A**

Abert's squirrel, 252–53
Allegheny woodrat, 268–69
alligator, American, 68–69
American alligator, 68–69
American pika, 220–21
American robin, 140–41
amphibians, 34–51
antelope, pronghorn, 312–13
arctic fox, 152–53
arctic ground squirrel, 242–43
armadillo, 146–47
Atlantic loggerhead turtle,
  62–63
avians, 70–141
avocet, 118–19

**B**

badger, 200–201
bald eagle, 92–93
bannertail kangaroo rat,
  286–87
bears, 172–79
beaver, 290–91
bighorn sheep, 314–15
birds. See avians
bison, 300–301
black bear, 172–73
black-billed magpie, 136–37
black-footed ferret, 192–93
black-tailed jackrabbit, 214–15
blacktail prairie dog, 230–31
blue grouse, 94–95
blue jay, 132–33
boar, wild, 298–99
bobcat, 164–65
bobwhite, 104–5
boreal toad, 40–41
brush cottontail, 210–11

bullfrog, 50–51
bushy-tailed woodrat, 262–63

**C**

California ground squirrel,
  238–39
California gull, 122–23
California quail, 106–7
Canada goose, 88–89
Canada lynx, 166–67
canids, 148–59
caribou, 304–5
chickaree squirrel, 256–57
chipmunks, 244–49
chorus frog, 44–45
coastal brown bear, 176–77
coati, 182–83
collared lemming, northern,
  274–75
collared peccary "javelina,"
  296–97
Colorado chipmunk, 246–47
common loon, 70–71
common raven, 138–39
coot, 112–13
cormorant, double-crested,
  74–75
cottontail rabbits, 206–13
coyote, 156–57
crabs, 30–33
crane, sandhill, 114–15
crow, 130–31

**D**

deer, 306–9
deer mouse, 260–61
desert cottontail, 212–13
double-crested cormorant,
  74–75

Douglas' squirrel, 256–57
duck, mallard, 84–85

**E**
eagles, 92–93
eastern chipmunk, 248–49
eastern cottontail rabbit,
  206–7
eastern gray squirrel, 250–51
eastern newt (red eft phase),
  34–35
eastern woodrat, 268–69
elk, 310–11

**F**
felids, 160–71
fence lizard, 52–53
feral hog, 298–99
ferret, black-footed, 192–93
fiddler crab, 30–31
fisher, 194–95
flicker, northern, 128–29
flying squirrel (northern and
  southern), 258–59
fox, 148–55
Franklin's ground squirrel,
  236–37
frogs, 44–51

**G**
goat, mountain, 320–21
golden eagle, 92–93
goose, Canada, 88–89
gopher, northern pocket,
  278–79
gray fox, 150–51
gray jay, 134–35
gray squirrel, eastern,
  250–51
great blue heron, 78–79
green-backed heron, 76–77
grizzly bear, 178–79

ground squirrel, 234–35
grouse, 94–99
gulls, 120–23

**H**
hare, snowshoe, 218–19
hawk, red-tailed, 90–91
herons, 76–79
herring gull, 120–21
hispid pocket mouse, 280–81
hoary marmot, 228–29
hog, feral, 298–99
hoofed mammals, 296–321
horseshoe crab, 32–33

**I**
insectivores, 144–45
invertebrates, 30–33

**J**
jackrabbits, 214–17
jaguar, 170–71
jaguarundi, 160–61
"javelina," collared peccary,
  296–97
jays, 132–35
jumping mouse, 276–77

**K**
kangaroo rats, 284–87
kit fox, 154–55
Kodiak bear, 176–77

**L**
lagomorphs, 206–21
least chipmunk, 244–45
lemming, northern collared,
  274–75
leopard frog, 48–49
lesser scaup, 86–87
lion, mountain, 168–69
lizards, 52–59

loggerhead turtle, Atlantic,
  62–63
long-tailed vole, 270–71
long-tailed weasel, 186–87
loon, common, 70–71
lynx, Canada, 166–67

**M**
magpie, black-billed, 136–37
mallard duck, 84–85
marmot, 224–25, 228–29
marsupial, 142–43
marten, 188–89
meadow vole, 272–73
Mexican woodrat, 266–67
mice. See mouse
mink, 190–91
moose, 302–3
mountain beaver, 222–23
mountain cottontail rabbit,
  208–9
mountain goat, 320–21
mountain lion, 168–69
mouse, 260–61, 276–77,
  280–83
mule deer, 308–9
muskox, 318–19
muskrat, 292–93
mustelids, 186–205
mute swan, 82–83

**N**
newt, eastern (red eft phase),
  34–35
northern collared lemming,
  274–75
northern flicker, 128–29
northern pocket gopher,
  278–79
nutria, 288–89

**O**
ocelot, 162–63
opossum, 142–43
Ord's kangaroo rat, 284–85
otter, river, 196–97
owl, 126–27

**P**
painted turtle, 64–65
peccary "javelina," collared,
  296–97
pelican, white, 72–73
pheasant, ring-necked,
  100–101
pika, American, 220–21
pine squirrel, 254–55
plains pocket mouse, 282–83
pocket gopher, northern,
  278–79
pocket mouse, plains, 282–83
polar bear, 174–75
porcupine, 294–95
prairie dog, blacktail, 230–31
prairie lizard, 52–53
procyonids, 180–85
pronghorn antelope, 312–13
ptarmigan, 102–3

**Q**
quail, 106–9

**R**
rabbits, 206–13. See also lagomorphs
raccoon, 184–85
rats, 284–87
raven, common, 138–39
red fox, 148–49
red squirrel, 254–55
red-tailed hawk, 90–91
reptiles, 52–69
ring-necked pheasant,

100–101
ringtail, 180–81
river otter, 196–97
roadrunner, 124–25
robin, American, 140–41
rock squirrel, 240–41
rodents, 222–95
ruffed grouse, 98–99

**S**
sagebrush lizard, 54–55
salamanders, 36–39
sandhill crane, 114–15
sandpiper, spotted, 116–17
scaled quail, 108–9
scaup, lesser, 86–87
sheep, 314–17
shorthorned lizard, 56–57
shrews, 144–45
skunk, 202–5
snake, 66–67
snapping turtle, 60–61
snowshoe hare, 218–19
spotted frog, 46–47
spotted salamander, 38–39
spotted sandpiper, 116–17
spotted skunk, 204–5
spruce grouse, 96–97
squirrels, 232–43, 252–59
striped skunk, 202–3
swans, 80–83
swift fox, 154–55

**T**
"tassle-eared" squirrel, 252–53
Texas horned lizard, 58–59

thinhorn sheep, 316–17
thirteen-lined ground squirrel,
  232–33
tiger salamander, 36–37
toads, 40–43
trumpeter swan, 80–81
turkey, 110–11
turtles, 60–65

**U**
ursids, 172–79

**V**
voles, 270–73

**W**
weasel, long-tailed, 186–87
white-footed mouse, 260–61
white pelican, 72–73
white-tailed deer, 306–7
white-tailed jackrabbit, 216–17
white-throated woodrat,
  264–65
wild boar, 298–99
wolf, 158–59
wolverine, 198–99
woodchuck, 226–27
Woodhouse's toad, 42–43
woodrats, 262–69

**Y**
yellow-bellied marmot, 224–25

## About the author

James Halfpenny has searched for dinosaur tracks in Colorado and Montana, followed iguanas in Ecuador, hiked seal trails in Antarctica, trailed wildlife in Tanzania and Kenya, studied endangered species on China's Tibet-Qinghai plateau, tracked brown bears and raccoon dogs in Japan, chased kangaroo tracks in Australia, and researched the polar bears of Hudson Bay and Greenland. Since 1961 he has taught outdoor and environmental education for a vast array of schools and organizations, including the Smithsonian, National Outdoor Leadership School, Outward Bound, the Appalachian Mountain Club, the Wilderness Society, the National Wildlife Federation, Defenders of Wildlife, and the National Audubon Society. He has trained National Park rangers in tracking techniques and his research has also taken him to Antarctica, Japan, and all over North America. Halfpenny was featured, with Australian aborigines, Kalahari Bushmen, and Alaskan Inuit, in a documentary about the loss of native tracking skills shown on the Discovery Channel. He is a past field director and project coordinator for the University of Colorado's Institute of Arctic and Alpine Research. He is also the senior author of the *Scats and Tracks* series (FalconGuide). He lives just outside Yellowstone National Park in Gardiner, Montana.

## About the illustrator

Todd Telander is a freelance natural science illustrator and wildlife artist. He studied biology and environmental studies at the University of California, Santa Cruz, where he became interested in illustration. His work appears in Falcon's *America's 100 Most Wanted Birds, Birder's Dictionary, A Field Guide to Cows,* and *A Field Guide to Pigs,* as well as in museums, galleries, and private collections. Todd lives in Walla Walla, Washington, with his wife, Kirsten, a writer, and their two sons, Miles and Oliver.